Planning for
Power Advertising

Planning for
Power Advertising

A user's manual for
students and practitioners

Anand Bhaskar Halve

Response Books
A division of Sage Publications
New Delhi/Thousand Oaks/London

First published in 2005 by

Response Books
A division of Sage Publications India Pvt Ltd
B-42, Panchsheel Enclave
New Delhi 110 017

Sage Publications Inc	**Sage Publications Ltd**
2455 Teller Road	1 Oliver's Yard, 55 City Road
Thousand Oaks, California 91320	London EC1Y 1SP

Published by Tejeshwar Singh for Response Books, typeset in 11/13 pts Souvenir by Innovative Processors, New Delhi, and printed at Chaman Enterprises, New Delhi.

Library of Congress Cataloging-in-Publication Data

Halve, Anand Bhaskar, 1955-
    Planning for power advertising: a user's manual for students and practitioners/Anand Bhaskar Halve.
        p. cm.
    Includes index.
    1. Advertising. 2. Advertising—India. I. Title.

HF5823.H3135 2005   659.1—dc22   2005019506

ISBN: 0–7619–3354–9 (PB)   81–7829–549–0 (PB)

Production Team: Anupama Purohit, R.A.M. Brown and Santosh Rawat

To my father, B.K. Halve,
for helping me learn the value of an unbounded interest
in everything in life,
an enquiring, curious mind
and the joy of discovering the 'pieces that fit'.

Factors that are invaluable in advertising.
Not to mention the rest of one's life.

Contents

List of Figures

List of Tables

Preface

This book has grown out of the notes, presentations, material and concepts I have used for workshops and seminars with students of advertising at Mudra Institute of Communication, Ahmedabad, the Indian Institute of Management, Ahmedabad, and other management schools.

My sessions at these schools revealed that, while the number of students interested in advertising is growing, there is a paucity of India-focused material to help them understand and appreciate the principles and process of creating powerful advertising. In the years gone by, it was enough to study what had happened in developed markets, especially the USA, and use those learnings as a template for what had to be done here. However, as the recent experience of several international companies has shown, the Indian market is unique in many ways; merely transplanting the seeds of lessons learnt abroad does not assure a rich harvest!

It is tempting, in such a context, to attempt to write an 'Everything you wanted to know about advertising in India' book. Many books have attempted to cover such an expanded canvas, but failed to do justice to specialized areas such as media planning and advertising research. On the other hand, to cover all these subjects in depth would require several volumes, not all of which would interest a particular individual.

Which brings me to the question I asked myself: Who is the book meant for? And what would be most useful to its readers? The answers not only led to the structure and content of the book, but also helped me clarify some of my own beliefs about advertising.

The first question that posed itself was: At what level to pitch it? As with preparing a presentation for a Seminar or Industry forum, any attempt to simultaneously address both the 'MD and the MT' (Management Trainee), falls in no man's land, and usually results in disappointing both. I have therefore focussed on the group that I call *the serious beginner*: this includes people in the formative stages of a career involving advertising; from students of advertising at a post-graduate level to people in the first five years of their careers in advertising and marketing.

Second, I believe that *advertising is a field in which there is no 'Single Right Answer'*. Different advertising solutions to a problem are possible, and the development of sound and powerful advertising stems more from an internalization of *an approach and process of thinking*, rather than formulae or mantras that promise success. The book is designed to help develop a process of thinking that is not formulaic, rigid, checklist-based, but *an informed-intuitive thinking process*. I liken this to the way a great chef cooks food: He doesn't work from a recipe book every time, but the principles of good cookig are so deeply internalised in him, he will never do something that curdles milk!

Third, I believe *Advertising is learnt, not taught,* and therefore the book is written in a way that engages the users' mind. The examples discussed— of what worked and what did not—are meant as stimuli to encourage the users to apply their mind, not as bases to derive theorems or immutable rules of advertising.

The field of advertising draws its 'raw material' from all of life, and no book can teach a person what to look out for. This book will not compensate for an unseeing eye or an un-inquisitive mind. But for those who are observing and trying to understand people and society, it will have helped them to develop a way of approaching an advertising problem, and a sense of the variables that are important, which leads to impactful advertising solutions.

The book, like all human works, is influenced and enriched by the interactions I have had with professional colleagues, clients, academics and bright students. Their views and questions have helped me refine my own thoughts and ideas.

Acknowledgements

My thanks go out to Prof. Abhinandan Jain at the Indian Institute of Management, Ahmedabad (IIMA); and the faculty and Prof. Kulkarni (ex-Director) at Mudra Institute of Communications, Ahmedabad (MICA); who have invited me to conduct workshops at IIMA and MICA, and created the opportunities for which I had to prepare the discussion material which led to this book. Thanks to Prof. Abhinandan Jain for also reading an earlier version of the book and his very helpful suggestions.

I would especially like to mention Kiran Khalap, my colleague at *chlorophyll,* in this context. Kiran is a very unusual Creative Director: he actually likes to understand the 'science' of advertising! Discussions with him have contributed significantly to helping me clarify my thinking.

Thanks also to my colleague Sunil Deshpande for creating the figures and charts, as well as for his help in improving the quality of the images of advertisements and Keshav Pilankar for his help with the storyboards of the TV commercials displayed in this book.

My heartfelt thanks to Chapal Mehra, Managing Editor, Response Books, who seeded the thought of this book in my mind. Without his help and guidance through unfamiliar publishing terrain, this book would not have been possible.

And finally to the *chanawalas* and the taxi drivers, the liftmen and *chowkidars*, the flower children and the flower-seller girls at traffic signals, the customers at Gokul behind the Taj and the barflies at the Taj President, the swingers in the pubs and the girls in dance-bars, the people from Page 3 and the people no one writes about, and everyone in between, who helped me learn that the 'raw material' for advertising, like the Truth in the *X-Files*, is 'out there'!

CHAPTER 1

Setting the Context

Thinking About What is a Strong Brand

Overview

Amitabh Bachchan is reportedly paid more than the cost of a Maybach by numerous advertisers, to be their brand ambassador. And they don't even get to keep him. Now, that is a strong brand!

This opening chapter is intended to set a backdrop to the specific step-by-step process—which we will begin in the next chapter—which will enable you to create powerful advertising that helps to build strong brands. In this chapter we will look at four key areas. First, we will see that the way in which the overall market context has changed, the highly competitive markets that we see today, the mergers and acquisitions which have become commonplace and the relaxation of controls on business in general are actually very recent developments. This is an important aspect of the Indian market which is necessary to understand to appreciate why there are relatively few indigenous brands with sharply developed associations and images; the fact is the brand-building efforts have not really been at work for very long. Second, we will look briefly at the international developments that reflected the appreciation of the value of brands. Third, we will look at some theoretical constructs related to the concept of brand equity, and at ways in which we can apply this concept in a practical way. And finally, we will see that brand strength is not a permanent status that a brand achieves; rather, it is a position that is constantly under attack and even the largest brands are not immune to challenges to their strength in the market, and more importantly in the consumers' mind and heart.

When you walk into a supermarket today, you see a wide range of brands in practically every category on the store shelves. When you switch on your TV set, there is a good chance that your cable service provider has a bouquet of more than 100 channels to offer. There are huge shopping malls coming up in city after city, which are changing the look of the urban landscape and changing shopping habits. And there are over 50 million mobile phones beeping around the country.

Looking at all these, it is difficult to remember just how recent these developments are. Consider events less than two decades ago. The 1980s were marked by a series of incidents that had important implications for Corporate India. The decade marked the somewhat reluctant, somewhat struggling change towards liberalization, and the consumer and brand-oriented economy of today. Here are some interesting highlights:

1985

- R. P. Goenka's attempt to acquire Dunlop India runs into trouble with the RBI.
- Sam Pitroda sets up the Centre for Development of Telematics C-DOT to develop an indigenous telephone switching system.
- Delicensing in the pharmaceuticals sector is extended to 82 bulk drugs and related drug formulations.
- M.R. Chhabria officially acquires control over Shaw Wallace, purchasing a 38.74 per cent stake from Sime Darby Behard.

1986

- Swraj Paul's attempts to acquire Escorts and DCM are foiled by the intervention of the financial institutions.
- The FIs oust Shaw Wallace Chairman and keep M.R. Chhabria out of the AGM.

1987

- S.K. Birla takes over battery-maker Chloride India from Chloride plc.
- The Hindujas acquire Ashok Leyland from Rover Motors of the UK, beating Rahul Bajaj.
- The first mutual fund, SBI Mutual fund, enters the market with its MRIS-87 scheme.
- M.R. Chhabria acquires Mather & Platt, Hindustan Dorr-Oliver, and Falcon Tyres.

1988

- The Securities & Exchange Board of India is set up to regulate the capital markets.
- The first shampoo sachet is launched by Velvette International.
- Manufacturing of telecom equipment for switching and transmission is privatised.

1989

- ○ The RPG group acquires the Calcutta Electric Supply Corporation.
- ○ The UB group CEO, Vijay Mallya, acquires Jenson & Nicholson in a pound 17 million overseas deal.

1990

- ○ VXL acquires Saurashtra Chemicals.
- ○ The UB group acquires a controlling interest in Mangalore Chemicals & Fertilisers.

One can almost see the business environment change before our eyes in this brief glance at events in corporate India! And the pace has only accelerated in more recent years. We have seen the consolidation in industries such as the cellular phone industry and we have seen the emergence of entire new industries such as the BPO industry. We have seen brands such as Thums Up, Limca and Mangola sold to MNCs. And we have seen a host of businessmen who were content to sell commodities or to do third-party manufacturing for export turn towards the launch of branded products: witness the emergence of brands such as Provogue in apparel, Kohinoor in rice, Haldiram's in snack foods, The Living Room in furniture, and so many others. They all point to an increased realization among Indian businessmen that strong brands are the path to wealth creation.

THE EMERGENCE OF THE IMPORTANCE OF BRANDS AND BRAND EQUITY

And even as the corporate battles were being fought over the tangible assets of companies such as Dunlop and Shaw Wallace in India, there were a few major developments that occurred in the United States of America in the 1980s, which heralded the arrival of the concept of the 'intangible value' of brands.

Let us briefly recall some of the most important cases, which demonstrated the idea that strong brands represented wealth.

Phillip Morris paid US$13 billion—600 per cent more than the book value—to acquire the consumer brands of Kraft Inc. in the US.

Kohlberg Kravis Roberts (KKR) paid US$25 billion in 1988 to take over RJR Nabisco, of which eighty per cent was paid for the value of the brands and other intangible assets (the balance sheet equity was $5.8 billion).

Grand Metropolitan acquired the Pillsbury brands for $5.5 billion, 50 per cent over the market capitalization.

These events brought 'brands' on to centre stage, and so began the search for ways to *define* brand equity, to measure it and to develop processes and methodologies to *build* brand equity.

The Nabisco, Kraft and other mega-deals established that brands with strong equity, represented economic value. Here are recent assessments of which are the world's most valuable brands, as reported by Interbrand, one of the pioneers and leaders in the area of brand valuation.

Table 1.1: Ranking of the world's most valuable brands ($ billion)

		2004	2003	2002
1	Coca-Cola	67.39	70.45	69.64
2	Microsoft	61.37	65.17	64.09
3	IBM	53.79	51.77	51.19
4	GE	44.11	42.34	41.31
5	INTEL	33.50	31.11	30.86
6	Disney	27.11	28.04	29.26
7	McDonald's	25.00	24.70	26.38
8	Nokia	24.04	29.44	29.97
9	Toyota	22.67	20.78	19.45
10	Marlboro	22.18	22.18	24.15

Source: Brandchannel.com

Brand valuations on these lines for Indian brands are not available, but if one uses the 'Trust' in brands as a *partial* indicator of the value of a brand, here is how Indian brands stack up.

Table 1.2: Ranking of India's most trusted brands

1	Colgate
2	Dettol
3	Pond's
4	Lux
5	Pepsodent
6	Tata Salt
7	Britannia
8	Rin
9	Surf
10	Close-up

Source: Brand Equity, *The Economic Times*, 17 December 2003.

In this table, we have considered one of the important aspects of brand equity: Trust. It is also important to think about what its other components are. But first, let us address the question of what we exactly mean by brand equity.

Although the term 'brand equity' has been used widely for over two decades, you will find a wide variation in the way professionals understand and use it. To check your own understanding of the concept, take a moment and write down *your* definition of brand equity.

Done? Good. Now, did you have a clear definition in mind? Or did you struggle a bit, as you tried to pin down exactly what 'brand equity' means to you?

If you did, don't worry, you are not alone. Consider some of the definitions of brand equity, which were presented in one of the early seminars on the subject organized by the American Marketing Institute and at the Marketing Science Institute of the USA.

> *'A function of associations, in the consumer's mind, with the brand name.'*
> *'The added value with which the brand endows a product.'*
> *'The cost a new entrant would have to incur to achieve the same share.'*

You will see that there is a strong *financial* orientation to some of these definitions. This is not surprising, since at that time, the main purpose of studying brand equity was the valuation of brands. This led to definitions with measurables such as cost, and market share. The definitions, which stepped away from that perspective on the other hand, such as the first definition quoted above, offered less clarity.

One of the seminal attempts to clarify the concept was Prof. David Aaker's *Managing Brand Equity*, first published in 1991. He wrote: 'Brand equity is a set of assets and liabilities linked to a brand, its name and symbol, that add to or subtract from the value provided by a product or service to a firm and/or that firm's customers.' (David A. Aaker, *Managing Brand Equity*, The Free Press, a division of Macmillan, New York, p 15)

Not only did he attempt to define brand equity, he also attempted to analyze it in terms of its components. But perhaps most importantly, he brought in a customer orientation, rather than one concerned with only valuation: 'Brand equity... add(s) to the value provided to a... firm's customers.' What follows is the diagrammatic representation of brand equity developed by Prof. Aaker.

In another model the core values of a brand are identified; that is, the set of values and meanings, which are intrinsic to and, in fact, *define* the brand; these are the elements of the brand, which must be preserved and protected.

Figure 1.1: David A. Aaker's diagrammatic representation of the components of brand equity

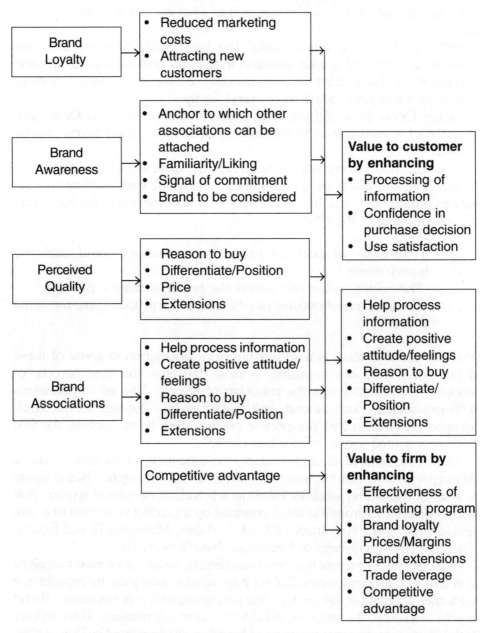

Source: David A. Aaker, *Managing Brand Equity,* The Free Press, a division of Macmillan, New York

Around this core, you can study the associations that *enhance* and strengthen the core of the brand, and on the other hand, those that take away from or weaken the core, and may need correction.

You also study the characteristics of the brand or images that are associated with the brand, but which do not add any significant value. And at the other end the associations or images which are important to consumers but which the brand does not possess.

BRAND EQUITY: FROM THEORY TO PRACTICE

Prof. Aaker's model and other models of brand equity that are in use, provide very useful frameworks to understand brands, and help to identify the areas in which the brand managers must plan their next steps. However, on a practical note, I believe that there are relatively few companies, which regularly conduct research to measure and track brands on these bases.

Think of a brand you work on, or are familiar with, and ask yourself these questions.

Do you know the extent of loyalty your brand commands?
What is the price elasticity of your brand?
What are the associations with your brands?
Which ones are stronger than others?

These are the kind of questions implicit in the models of brand equity. In the absence of these data, how would one assess the strength of a brand?

And because many companies, and thus many practitioners have to work without these data, I have considered and developed metrics based on data which are (a) fairly easily available or can be estimated relatively easily and (b) conceptually reflect a brand's underlying customer acceptance (i.e. its brand equity).

Undoubtedly such an effort leaves out some aspects of Brand Equity as proposed in Prof. Aaker's comprehensive model, but I believe that just as there is a need for a conceptually comprehensive approach, it is important to have measures which may be less comprehensive, but can be applied by most practitioners.

One can approach this by looking at the variables proposed by Prof. Aaker, as being of two types: *Input* variables, and *Output* variables. Brand awareness, associations, etc. may be considered 'input' variables, which the brand owner can affect directly. Through increased advertising spends, for example.

Others such as 'Brand loyalty' or market share are what might be termed 'output' variables, in that they are the *result* of interaction between the efforts of the brand owner, the efforts of other brands and their activities, and the customers' response to all of these.

I suggest using two simple measures to look at brands at an overall input and output level. It must be noted that these are not intended to substitute the more comprehensive set of measures; rather they are surrogates to be used as thumb rule measures of the strength of a brand, when one does not have extensive research on brand equity.

The two variables that I arrived at are based on data, which would be used every year, for every brand, in every company.

The first measure relates to the *input* that is applied i.e. the advertising and sales promotion support provided to a brand.

The second measure relates to the *output* achieved by the brand i.e. the sales of the brand.

These variables are:

1. *Input-Related Variable: The advertising support in money terms put behind the brand to maintain or grow sales.* This includes the spend on mass media advertising, promotions, Direct Marketing activities, Events, sponsorships, Internet advertising, in-film placements, and so on—all the tools the company uses to intervene with customers and prospects to build preference and loyalty for the brand.

2. *Output-Related Variable: The sales achieved (whether in Rupees or tonnes or kilolitres).* This is finally, the goal of building strong brands.

   There is a lot that has been written about how advertising does not impact sales, and that it affects intermediate variables such as awareness, brand image, and so on. It is true that advertising does not always affect sales directly i.e. in a one to one correspondence. However, it must eventually, even though it may act indirectly, help to drive sales. (More pertinently, we are at the moment looking at the strength of brands—and there is no such thing as a strong brand that does not sell!)

Let us take these two variables and construct measures, which we can use to appreciate the strength of a brand. To make this exercise more meaningful, take a moment to think of a real brand. Preferably, it should be a brand that you yourself work on, a brand that you are knowledgeable about. If not, consider any brand that you are at least reasonably familiar with.

INPUT-RELATED MEASURE: BRAND INPUT MULTIPLIER

The first measure I propose is a simple operational one, which I have called the Brand Input Multiplier, and is a measure of the power of the brand's communication. This considers the inputs being used in interventions for the brand and looks at how hard they are working, the assumption being that *the inputs will work harder for a strong brand.*

We may assume broadly, at least for most advertised categories, that the advertising *inputs* and *outputs* have a relatively short time lag which may be assumed to take place within, say, a one-year period. (This is not to say, even for a moment, that *all the intangible effects of advertising occur within a year.* But at the moment, we are only considering simple and more importantly, practical, ways to get a broad *assessment of the strength of brands.*)

The Brand Input Multiplier can then be defined as:

$$\frac{SOM}{SOV}$$

(Where, SOM = exit market share i.e. market share of brand at the end of
　　　　　the year, and

　　　　SOV = share of voice of the advertising by the brand during
　　　　　the year)

Work out the Brand Input Multiplier for your brand over the past couple of years. If the figure you arrive at is around 1.00, it would mean that the brand basically is about *as strong as the average brand in the market,* since it shows that each percentage point of share of voice is 'delivering' about one percentage point of market share.

A Brand Input Multiplier, which is significantly higher than 1.00 indicates a stronger brand than average, while a Brand Input Multiplier significantly below 1.00, is an indication of the weakness of the brand.

Take a few minutes to carry out this exercise for your brand. And for your most powerful competing brand. [For a more comprehensive measure, the SOV may be calculated on the basis of *total* expenditure on advertising and sales promotions, not just mass media advertising. For a more mathematically refined measure, mass media spends can be adjusted for 'equivalent Gross Rating Points' or 'Gross Rating Seconds' to factor in the role of different reach and durations of communications on television, and so on. A detailed discussion of refinements to this methodology is beyond the scope of this book. But even a simple measure based on total expenditure on advertising and sales promotions will work as a rough and ready indicator].

OUTPUT-RELATED MEASURE: DECAY RATE

I have defined the measure 'Decay Rate' as the rate at which the sales of a brand will drop, if there is no effort to intervene in the marketplace and affect customer choice. The Decay Rate is a measure of the *vulnerability* of your brand.

Think about your brand. Index its current sales at 100. (It does not matter whether you consider sales in rupees, tonnes, or any other unit.) Now ask yourself: what would the sales of your brand be after one year *if you stopped all advertising and promotion activity*? (You can assume that all other competing brands will continue their advertising and marketing support activity unaffected by your decision.)

What would you expect the sales of your brand to be if you continued the same way for another year? And after yet another year?

Now think about your most powerful competing brand. What do you think will be the effects of following the same practice, on your most powerful competing brand?

Plot your projected figures on a graph with the indexed sales on the Y-axis and years on the X-axis.

Figure 1.2 is an example of what such a plot might look like, using hypothetical data. The projected sales for Brand A starting with an Index value of 100 over the next three years are: 90, 81, 73. The projected sales for Brand B, again starting with an Index value of 100 over the next three years are: 85, 72, 61. On a year-to-year basis, Brand A has a Decay Rate of 10 per cent p.a., while brand B has a Decay Rate of 15 per cent p.a.

Figure 1.2: Decay rates for two hypothetical brands

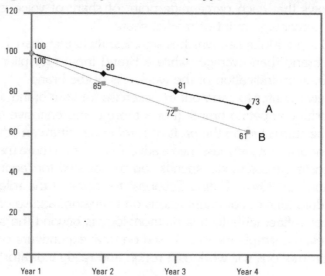

THE CHALLENGE OF BUILDING STRONG BRANDS

Whether you actually took the trouble to construct the Brand Input Multiplier measure, or the Brand Decay Rate measure and or not, just considering these measures would have given you a feel for the strength of your brand.

If you have a high Decay Rate, and have a low Brand Input Multiplier, you are looking at a *weak* brand. If you have a low Decay Rate, and have a high Brand Input Multiplier (i.e. each percentage point share of voice is working harder) on the other hand, you are looking at a *strong* brand.

The process described in this book is designed to help you create the foundations for advertising to build strong brands. And the way to do it is by remaining consumer-focused. It is also important to remember that a strong brand is not something that is 'built' once, like a building. It is rather something that you build, and then continuously work at to maintain, like a strong body!

Before going on to Chapter 2, consider the ranks held by some of India's most well known brands over the years, and how fragile brand strength can be (you can register yourself at *www.aandm.com* and access the Brand Diary, to look at fairly detailed analyses of what these brands did over the period over which this data was collated.)

Table 1.3: Change in ranking of India's top brands

Brand Ranks: A&M Top Brands

	1992	1993	1994	1995	1996	1997	1998	1999	2001
Colgate	1	1	1	1	1	2	1	1	1
Liril	NA	NA	33	29	52	36	53	49	52
Lifebuoy	NA	5	4	3	13	15	6	5	5
Dettol	4	3	3	8	3	NA	10	3	2
Amul	18	19	26	24	18	33	24	2	42
Pond's	11	13	9	11	3	6	3	11	18
Ariel	NA	29	30	27	21	18	19	6	22
BPL	NA	59	NC	55	40	35	40	31	44

NA = Not Available, NC = Not considered for ranking in that year.

Source: www.aandm.com

The only brand which has not shown wide variation in ranking is Colgate, and to some extent Dettol, barring two years when it dipped.

On the other hand look at Amul: It climbed from a rank of 33 in 1997 and 24 in 1998, to a rank of 2 in 1999, only to fall to 42 in the next year! Ariel clawed its way up the ranks over five years, from number 30 in 1994

Figure 1.3: TV commercial: Colgate toothpaste

A man comes and clowns in front of her "*...door se log aaye par usey hansa na paaye*". (Translation: People came from far away, but no one could make her smile)

One man saw the problem. "*Dentist se darti ho na?*" (Translation: You are scared of the dentist, aren't you?)

VO: *Ek thi Rajkumari jo kabhi hasti nahi thi...* (Translation: Once upon a time there was a princess who never used to smile...)

Despite all efforts, she refused to smile

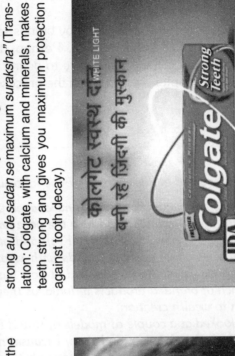

मॉक्सिमम सुरक्षा

Calcium *aur* minerals *yukt* Colgate *daant banaye strong aur de sadan se* maximum *suraksha"* (Translation: Colgate, with calcium and minerals, makes teeth strong and gives you maximum protection against tooth decay.)

कोलगेट स्वस्थ दांत, बनी रहे जिंदगी की मुस्कान

VO: Colgate. *Swast daant, bani rahe zindagi ki muskaan.* (Translation: Colgate. Healthy teeth, makes your smile stay for life).

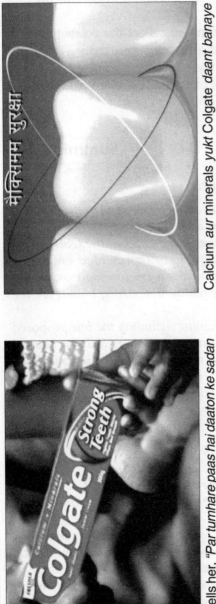

He tells her, *"Par tumhare paas hai daaton ke sadan se best suraksha"* (Translation: But you have the best protection against tooth decay.)

The little girl smiles as her fears disappear.

to number 6 in 1999, only to slip all the way down to 22 in the following year. The ranking of Pond's has been on a roller coaster throughout the decade.

The variation in the ranks held by brands seems to reflect the volatility in the stock prices of some brands. Perhaps there was more than a little prescience in using the term *equity* to define the strengths of brands!

In the next chapter, we will begin the process of actually developing Power Advertising.

Summing Up

The key points covered in this chapter are the following:

1. *We saw the major changes that have taken place in recent years in the business environment in India. And how the pace has accelerated.*
2. *We reviewed how the Nabisco, Kraft and other mega-deals in the USA, in the 1980s, established that brands with strong equity represented enormous economic value. And we looked at how businessmen are turning towards the launch of branded products in India, as they realize that strong brands are the path to wealth creation.*
3. *We looked at a couple of models of Brand Equity, including the one proposed by Prof. David Aaker, and then, because many practitioners in India have to work without the data required to apply these models in totality, we considered metrics based on data which are (a) fairly easily available and (b) reflect a brand's underlying customer acceptance (i.e. its brand equity).*
   We looked at two measures:

   ○ *The Brand Input Multiplier, defined as:*

   $$\frac{SOM}{SOV}$$

   Where, SOM=exit market share i.e. market share of brand at the end of the year, and SOV=share of voice of the advertising by the brand during the year
   We noted that a Brand Input Multiplier, which is significantly higher than 1.00 indicates a stronger brand than average, while a Multiplier significantly below 1.00, is an indication of the weakness of the brand.
   ○ *The 'Decay Rate' defined as the rate at which the sales of a brand will drop, if there is no effort to intervene in the marketplace and affect customer choice and that the Decay Rate is a measure of the vulnerability of a brand.*

4. *Finally, we noted the importance of remembering that a strong brand is not something that is 'built' once; but is, rather, something that you build, and then have to continuously work at to maintain.*

CHAPTER 2

Competition

The Changing Nature of Markets

Overview

Dialogue from Hindi film in 1985: Hamne tumhari beti ko kidnap kiya hai. Agar ladki zinda chahiye to 10 lakh rupiya lekar Versova beach aa jao. (Translation: We have kidnapped your daughter. If you want her back alive, bring 10 lakh rupees to Versova beach.)

Dialogue from Hindi film in 2004: Seth, bhai ne 50 crore maanga hai (Translation: Boss, the Don has demanded 50 crore rupees.)

(It is clear that everything has changed in the last two decades!)

India is a 5000-year-old civilization, and a 20-year-old market. Well, 20 years is obviously an exaggeration, but the changes in the market over the past two decades have been so great, one may well treat these as having ushered in a completely new era. All of us have heard and read about the changes that have taken place in recent years: the increase in the number of competing brands in almost every category, the easy availability of brands from all over the world and the changes in retailing with the emergence of supermarkets, malls, and departmental stores. All of which definitely make the market far more competitive.

However, there are some important dimensions to these developments and the changing nature of competition, which are not always seen in sharp focus. It is worth taking a moment to step back and understand these developments. Because they highlight some factors which were crucial in the development of marketing and communication strategies in this period. In this chapter, we will first look at the changes in the media scene, which created the right condition for reaching large audiences. Next we will look at how competition changes, with competition emerging not only from other brands in the category, but also from brands in other categories. And finally, we will look at the major directions that are defining the competitive context of brands.

A. FACILITATING COMPETITION: THE GROWTH OF MEDIA

The most fundamental aspect of change, which led to increased competition in the Indian marketplace, was the change in the *ability to reach* more prospective customers with your message. This capability only really came into the marketing and advertising tool-kit in India in the early 1980's. It happened thanks to the Asian Games, held in Delhi in 1982. Or more correctly, thanks to the way in which preparation for these games changed television in India. *Doordarshan*, the Government broadcaster, brought in on the one hand, colour transmission to television, and on the other, established a large network of Low Power Transmitters (LTPs) to take terrestrial transmission nationwide.

Table 2.1: Growth of reach of television in India

Growth of Doordarshan Network (1980 to 2002)

As on	PPC	HPT	LPT	VLPT	T	TT	CP (per cent)	CA (per cent)	Other Trans- mitters
1980	10	18	–	–	–	18	25	13.5	–
31.3.1983	10	23	20	–	–	43	26.4	15.4	1
31.3.1985	17	40	132	–	–	172	56.2	36.5	1
31.3.1987	17	46	148	3	–	197	70.3	46.8	2
31.3.1989	18	52	237	46	–	335	73.9	51.4	4
31.3.1990	18	55	374	72	18	519	76.3	54.5	4
31.3.1991	20	60	372	76	19	527	78.7	57.7	4
31.3.1993	25	67	372	80	23	542	82.9	63.5	4
31.3.1994	32	70	389	82	23	564	84.5	66.6	7
31.3.1995	34	74	478	100	20	672	85.1	67.8	27
31.3.1996	40	77	526	120	20	743	85.8	68.8	49
31.3.1997	41	82	596	170	20	868	87.1	69.2	53
31.3.1998	42	83	600	196	18	897	87.1	71.6	52
31.3.1999	46	84	654	228	18	984	87.6	72.9	57
31.3.2000	47	86	674	251	19	1030	87.9	74.8	60
31.3.2001	51	89	711	277	21	1098	88.9	76.3	92
1.6.2002	56	103	749	316	20	1188	89.6	77.5	126

Note: PPC: Programme Production Centre, T: Transposer, TT: Total Transmitters
CP: Coverage of Population, CA: Coverage of Area.

Source: Doordarshan India 2002

THE MASS MARKET WITHIN REACH

It is important to note that until the expansion of the TV transmission network, brands could not actually think of pan-Indian *mass consumer markets,* since there was no medium with nationwide reach that was available. With the network of transmitters expanding, the area coverage of television went up from 13.5 per cent of India in 1982, to 46.8 per cent by 1987. During the same period, the increase in the reach of television as a medium was even more dramatic: going up from coverage of 25 per cent of the population in 1980, to 70.3 per cent of the population in 1987. As an important consequence of this higher reach, brands could not only expand the scope of their operations as they expanded into markets across a much wider footprint than before, they could also seek economies of scale which allowed them to give even greater impetus to market development.

There was one other important element in the reach of television in the 80s: the fact that by using just a few high-reach television programs you could achieve TRPs that were almost 100 per cent! It was this fact that made television an incredibly cost-effective medium for advertising. Some of the programs, which delivered such audience, were *Chitrahaar/Chhayageet*, the Sunday Hindi feature film (and Tamil feature film in Tamil Nadu), and serials like *Hum Log* (1984), *Ramayana* (1987), and *Mahabharata* (1988). These economies of cost of reach via television also made mass media advertising *affordable to smaller players,* who could gain the salience and acceptability of 'well-known' brands.

Two brands which grabbed this opportunity and dramatically changed the competitive landscape of the categories in which they competed were Vicco (with its Vajradanti Toothpowder and Toothpaste and Vicco Turmeric Ayurvedic Cream) and Nirma in washing powders.

Without a cost-efficient medium that had an all-India reach, neither of these brands would have been able to build the kind of high awareness and trial that was fundamental to converting them from regional players to major national brands. Moreover, they served as path breakers to other brands that followed in their categories.

Figure 2.1: Pack design: Vicco Turmeric Ayurvedic Cream

'DON'T TELL ME—SHOW ME': THE POWER OF THE MOVING IMAGE

The changes in media reach, and the growth of television also had one other fundamental effect: By going beyond the limitations of literacy and education inherent in the print media, and bringing the power of the *moving image* into millions of homes, it *changed the basis of how people responded* to brands.

For example, Garden Silk Mills was able to move from being a relatively small player from Surat, to Vareli emerging as the definitive fashion icon in ladies wear.

Figure 2.2: Press advertisement: Vareli

The Vareli ad presented 'fashion photography' style work, possibly for the first time for an Indian brand.

The moving image also played an important role in the generic expansion of many categories. It allowed marketers to *demonstrate product usage* to expand small markets and create new ones. It is easy today to look down on these kinds of messages—from a perspective of awareness and knowledge of urban living—as simplistic, but it was this factor that allowed the creation of several new markets.

Let us consider just two examples.

Pioma Industries from Ahmedabad, created a new category: the soft drink concentrate. Compared to the existing alternatives offered by squashes and syrups, Pioma Industries *showed* the ease and economy of using their fruit drink concentrate. They did it well enough for the country to learn to say, 'I love you, Rasna.'

Figure 2.3: Press advertisement: Rasna

Similarly, in a situation where many people had never used a washing machine, and really had little idea of how one used it, Videocon *demonstrated* exactly how a washing machine worked ('it washes, it rinses, it even dries your clothes'). This may have seemed incredibly simple-minded to people who were used to the idea of washing machines, but it provided information to a lot of others who not so familiar, and created the market for washing machines.

The foregoing rearview-mirror look at the developments in media and marketing might appear to be of merely historical interest. However, in a very real sense, the developments in the television medium 'opened up' markets, ahead of the process of liberalization, which of course opened up markets in quite another sense. The experience with television should also sensitize us to observe changes taking place today, which might have similar far-reaching implications for reaching audiences. For instance, what are the likely effects of the growth of usage of SMS by youngsters? We have already seen their effect in the TV show, *Indian Idol*. How else could one exploit their potential? What about the increased use of Instant Messenger software? Or, of email? What about the use of FM radio? The possibilities are limited only by our ability to spot opportunities and our creativity in utilizing them.

With the expansion in markets and brand sales, came a rapid expansion in the *manufacturing capacities* in many industries, and the introduction of a plethora of new brands. Here are India's biggest brands as reported by Brand Equity. Most of these are less than 25 years old, and indicate the growth of the consumer products markets. (International brands have been deliberately left out from the list to focus on the growth of indigenous brands.)

Table 2.2: India's biggest brands

Rank	Brand	Turnover (Rs. Crore)
3	Thums Up	1688
9	Nirma	1092
11	Wheel	826
18	Fair & Lovely	640
24	Ghari	524
30	Fortune	395
31	Nima	395
32	Frooti	391
40	Breeze	313
41	Amul	311
46	Gemini	266
47	Dhara	262
51	Sundrop	238
54	Amul Spray	228
55	Santoor	214

Source: Brand Equity, *The Economic Times*, 21 Apr 2004

B. COMPETITION ACROSS CATEGORIES

With the growth of media, and the opportunities for market development being demonstrated by pioneers such as Nirma, Vicco and Rasna; it was inevitable that competitors would follow. However, there was more than just competition from 'like' products that came in. There was also competition *across product categories*, which had a significant effect on brands.

THE AGGREGATION AND FRAGMENTATION OF CATEGORIES

One of the basic reasons why practitioners sometimes miss the changes taking place around them, and get blindsided by them, is the way that *markets* are classically defined. Of course this was a point made by Theodore Levitt in his article 'Marketing Myopia', in the *Harvard Business Review*. It may well be the most-quoted thought in marketing. Here is what he wrote about the failure of the railroads in the USA to understand what business they were in:

> The railroads did not stop growing because the need for passenger and freight transportation declined. That grew. The railroads are in trouble today—not because the need is met by other means of transport (cars, trucks, airplanes, even telephones), but because it was not met by the railroads themselves. They let others take customers away from them because they assumed themselves to be in the railroad business rather than in the transportation business. The reason they defined their industry wrong was because they were railroad-oriented instead of transportation-oriented; they were product-oriented instead of customer-oriented.

This is a relevant place at which to also clarify what is a common source of confusion. Terms like 'markets', 'segments' and 'categories' are often used without rigorous clarity, and therefore – interchangeably. In order to avoid confusion, think of the following definitions, which capture the core meaning of these terms.

Market: Ideally as pointed out by T. Levitt, we should use this term with reference to *the purpose or need for which the consumer uses the product*. So for instance, we could speak of the 'hair care' market (which may include shampoos, hair-oils, hair dyes etc) or the 'non-alcoholic beverage' market (which may include carbonated as well as non-carbonated drinks in addition to fruit juices).

If one is looking at only product-level competition or practices, the term 'product category' may be more accurate to use than the term 'market'.

Product category: This defines *products which have a basic similarity, based on which customers are likely to group them in the short term:* the members of some product categories are easy to see, such as the 'coffee' category or the 'tea' category; others may be a little less obvious, such as the 'bottled soft drinks' category (does it include only carbonated drinks or does it include non-carbonated drinks like Mangola too?). The usage and understanding of these terms can have a significant bearing on how you see the competition for your brand, and thus how you plan its advertising, as we shall see below.

THE 'CROSS-OVER' PHENOMENON IN CATEGORIES

While we defined 'market' above in terms of consumer purpose, it is also important to note whether changes are taking place around us, which indicate a need to *define markets, which cut across product categories.*

If it is very clear that the competition is limited to a particular product type, one may use the term 'market' to refer to a group of similar products; for example one may refer to the 'colour-TV market' or the 'cola market'. However, this can be sometimes misleading because it keeps us from seeing other *threats, which are coming from outside such category-defined sets of products and brands.*

Consider this. In North India, where summers can be quite severe, do ceiling fans compete only with ceiling fans; or do they also compete with desert coolers?

Is *Bend it like Beckham* an Indian film made in the UK? Or, an English film for Indians? Or is it a film in English with some dialogues in Hindi, made for the Indian diaspora living in the UK?

The question really being asked is: do such questions prevent a more important realization that forced categorizations and 'either/or' choices keep us from seeing that the correct answer is, 'all of the above'? Perhaps *Bend it like Beckham* is just a film whose characters are Indians living in the UK, with the dialogues largely in English… just as *The King &I* is a film about an Englishwoman who went to China, with its dialogues largely in English?

Nonetheless, *Bend it like Beckham* was a milestone, and perhaps gave the term 'crossover' itself, wide currency.

This 'crossover' effect is another consequence of the growing competition in many markets.

Figure 2.4: Poster: *Bend it like Beckham*

Let's take two-wheelers. Until quite recently, the two-wheeler market was seen as clearly made up of 3 categories:

(a) *Motorcycles* were seen as 'manly' vehicles, not suitable for women, and as less fuel-efficient than scooters, more expensive in terms of initial cost, and not very safe (in spite of their larger wheel base, and better balance).

In sum: They were thought of as the two-wheeler of choice of the young, male roustabout.

(b) *Scooters* were the quintessential two-wheelers, better than motorcycles in terms of fuel economy, with a lower initial investment, and easier for women to ride (especially because of the 'step-through' frame).

In sum: Scooters were the family two-wheeler.

(c) *Mopeds* were the poor man's option. Far better than motorcycles or scooters in terms of fuel-economy and price, they were also easy to drive by man, woman, child or an aged person.

In sum: The only motorized vehicle option for those who couldn't afford a scooter or motorcycle.

But in 1985, Hero Honda introduced their 100cc bike with the four-stroke engine, with an amazing 80km/litre fuel economy, and the tag line: 'Fill it. Shut it. Forget it.'

This was an offer, which even the 'Chartered Accountant from Madurai', couldn't refuse! This 'crossover two-wheeler', a motorcycle with the fuel efficiency beyond anything even a scooter could provide, was the herald of a complete change in the structure of the two-wheeler market.

Consider these tables showing the production levels of scooters and motorcycles between 1993–94 and 2001–02

Table 2.3: Production of scooters—financial year (1993–94 to 2001–02)

Year	Manufacturers					Total
	BAL	KHML	LML	MSL	TVS	
1993–94	520793	70281	136813	113999	–	842407
1994–95	633675	89355	202001	105615	–	1030803
1995–96	714926	113531	238750	126620	30944	1224889
1996–97	710793	110751	278556	154356	58283	1312920
1997–98	640101	113525	314105	139834	71902	1279467
1998–99	623206	100422	333731	153602	104094	1315055
1999–00	594436	116790	275805	140530	131862	1259423
2000–01	356159	123304	168802	91739	139755	879759
2001–02	374135	108301	125470	60216	146421	870213

Abbr.: BAL: Bajaj Auto Ltd., KHML: Kinetic Honda Motors Ltd., LML: LML Limited. MSL: Maharashtra Scooters Ltd., TVS: TVS Motor Company Ltd.

Source: Society of Indian Automobile Manufacturers

This crossover effect led to a situation where Bajaj Auto, which had been the dominant two-wheeler brand in the 'scooter era', struggled for several years, as consumer preference shifted towards motorcycles. It took time for Bajaj Auto to get its act together; and it was able to rebuild market share only after developing strong offers in *motorcycles*.

Figure 2.5: Poster: Pulsar: 'Definitely Male'

**Table 2.4: Production of motorcycles—financial year
(1993–94 to 2001–02)**

Years	Manufacturers					Total
	BAL	HHML	REML	TVS	YML	
1993–94	134476	145248	16782	52589	113119	464750
1994–95	197919	182488	16377	86382	158467	647521
1995–96	238080	230081	21635	125661	187557	809087
1996–97	311134	268612	22829	167522	217352	988233
1997–98	313098	405040	17986	210629	179205	1125958
1998–99	373873	532529	24331	273461	183092	1204194
1999–00	431837	761210	23278	325319	252434	1541644
2000–01	548326	1034074	21432	358024	179519	2004266
2001–02	724397	1422112	24136	455224	238636	2961906

Abbr.: BAL: Bajaj Auto Ltd., YML: Yamaha Motor India (P) Ltd. HHML: Hero Honda Motors Ltd., TVS: TVS Motor Company Ltd., REML: Royal Enfield Motors Ltd.

Source: Society of Indian Automobile Manufacturers

The customer is today quite willing to 'crossover', as readily in the films he sees as in the products he buys, not really tied down to 'categories' defined in the marketing departments of companies. It raises the question of how exactly you should look at market data in planning for your brand.

Aggregation and Fragmentation of Categories

It is important to realise that even as the simple divisions between categories are breaking down, the 'constellation of competition' is also being redefined by other changes taking place in lifestyle, in product technology, and in usage habits.

Some of these developments have the effect of *creating greater aggregates*, in which competition takes place. For example, think of the change that has taken place in how you serve guests who drop into your home in the evening. Some years ago, the hostess might have asked, 'Would you care for some tea or coffee?' Today, there is much higher home-stocking of bottled beverages, and she might ask, 'Can I offer you tea or coffee. Or would you like a Pepsi?' The change in home-stocking of soft drinks has made tea, coffee and Pepsi 'competitors' in a new 'home consumption' aggregate.

In other cases, we are seeing the *fragmentation of a category* into sub-groups. For instance, in the case of wet milk (as opposed to powdered milk), we are seeing the emergence of two fragments: liquid milk, which is sold in pouches and long-life, homogenized milk, which is sold in aseptic packaging. Each has a different consumer profile, different buying and usage patterns and is not really considered 'competition' by users of the other type of milk.

As the next step toward understanding and internalizing these ideas, imagine you are responsible for building a brand of tea. Take a minute to think of *a specific brand in the market* as 'your brand'. Did that? Now look at the following chart and answer the question: whom am I competing with?

Consider the 'aggregation' effects first: is your brand competing with coffee in the hot beverage consumption context? Are changes taking place in preferences, due to which these are genuine 'alternatives'? Is this happening more or less in certain geographic areas?

Or going even further, in social contexts, for example, is tea competing with fruit juices, carbonated drinks, etc.?

The point is not as far-fetched as it might sound at first glance. It was only by looking at such aggregation effects, that the idea of iced tea could have been born. Very often, you will find that consumers have innovated product concepts well ahead of marketers—so keep watching what's happening in the real world!

On the other hand, there are 'fragmentation' effects that may also be taking place. For example, is the preference for different end-cup tea characteristics creating distinct competitive clusters of leaf and dust tea—or is this a categorization that is only used by marketers? What about the source of tea? Do people see Darjeeling teas as distinctly different from others?

Or consider changes in the delivery system for tea. Are tea bags leading to a perception of delivering a clearly *different type* of tea? Would competition for some consumers be therefore limited to brands, which offer the tea bag delivery system? (This is akin to saying that for some men, the shaving cartridge system vs the old two-edge blade is not really a choice: they will consider only those brands that offer the shaving cartridge delivery system.)

Create a copy of the following chart, consider the changing competitive context as you see it, and answer the question: whom am I competing with?

Table 2.5: Aggregation and fragmentation analysis for tea

Category Competition Chart

Product Substitutes considered: Beverage	Hot Beverages	Fruit Juices	Carbonated Drinks	Squashes, Syrups
Usage characteristic: Hot beverage	Tea	Coffee		
Aggregation Analysis				
Product	Tea			
Fragmentation Analysis				
Basis of classification: A	Leaf Tea	Dust Tea		
Basis of classification: B	Blended	Assam	Nilgiri	Darjeeling
Packaging/Delivery system	Carton	Pouch	Tea Bag	

The intention of this exercise was to show that it is not always very easy to see where exactly the competition—or the opportunity—might lie. And if you need proof, think back to the Nescafe advertising not long ago, which attempted to place coffee (Nescafe, of course) in the 'morning cup' use context, where it was targeting the large majority of Indians whose 'morning cup' beverage of choice is tea.

Here are a couple of assessment charts created for other products, as thought-starters.

SAMPLE ASSESSMENT OF CATEGORY CHANGES: PASSENGER CAR

In this example, we look at a passenger car, and consider the three dimensions, which could be creating *category level competitive challenges*: Usage characteristics, Bases of classification that consumers use along with the key product characteristics and the service/performance/delivery characteristics

Table 2.6: Sample assessment of category changes in cars

Dimension	Assesment of your brand	Changes likely to affect it	Competitive implications
Key Usage Characteristics	In-city conveyance: We are designed for urban usage	Increase in outstation travel (weekend trips)	−Expectation of rough road handling −Fuel economy will become more critical: will diesel models have an advantage? −Emergence of 'youth' or 'woman' segments? We are well-suited to tap into these trends
	Family transpor-tation: We can only seat 4 in comfort	Two-car families, single-individual usage	
Dominant Bases of Product Classification by Customers	Size and shape: Tall boy design	'Cross-over' vehicles which are 'hybrids' between SUVs and sedans	New set of 'consideration set' brands—whose imagery will need to be understood.
Service/ Performance/ Delivery Characteristics	Fuel efficiency: We have very high fuel efficiency	Price of petrol increases	Characteristic may become the *determinant* of choice rather than being just an 'important' criterion
		'Luxuries' becoming table stakes: radio, CD player, power steering, etc	What is our 'basic' offer? Will it put us in a different 'set' in the emerging scene?

SAMPLE ASSESSMENT OF CATEGORY CHANGES: INDIAN PRIVATE BANK

Table 2.7: Sample assessment of category changes in banks

Dimension	Assesment of your brand	Changes likely to affect It	Competitive implications
Key Usage Characteristics	Basic deposit of salaries, other income and with-drawal or issue of cheques for expenses	Greater interest in investments inclu-ding shares, mutual funds, etc.	–Competition from 'Investment advisory' companies –Less 'idle' funds in savings accounts: impact on cost of funds
	Depository accounts opened by large proportion of savings account holders	Active *pursuing* of depository business by Investment services companies	–Threat yes, but is there an oppor-tunity to grow depository accounts?
Basis of Product Classification by Customers	PSU banks, Indian private banks, Co-operative banks and MNC banks	MNC banks becoming more 'approachable' PSU banks also becoming more service oriented	Banks likely to compete as individual brands, rather than being 'clubbed' in earlier groups
Service/ Performance/ Delivery Characteristics	'All services at one place' becoming common consumer choice	Brings in compari-son with investment services	Non-banking companies entering competitive space-What is our image standing among this competitive set?

Now, think of the brand you are actually involved with, and assess which are the emerging market directions, which are likely to reshape your competitive landscape using the Action Point Format.

C. THE DIMENSIONS OF COMPETITION

We have seen some examples of the changes in competitive context that can take place at the category level. However, to plan the strategy for your brand, it is essential to understand the *different dimensions of competition,* which affect consumer choice and preference. These dimensions are important, within whatever group of products you have identified as the 'competing set' for your brand.

In many categories brand competitiveness comes from offering specialization or superiority built around a limited set of attributes or performance characteristics, which change relatively little over time. For example, in the case of detergents, these would be cleaning power/effectiveness, gentleness on clothes, stain removal, etc.

In milk beverages, the dominant territory is extra energy, growth and the nutrient content of the brand.

Yet there are categories in which the competitive landscape can change dramatically—often, in very unexpected ways. This challenges brands to create and also to face *new dimensions or directions of competition*. Here are some examples.

1. DIMENSION: PRICE SPECTRUM VS PRICE POINTS

Price is perhaps the most basic dimension along which we think of competition. So, for example you think of 'premium' soaps and 'popular' soaps. And much the same principle would apply, were you to think of readymade shirts, or packaged tea, or television sets. All the way to a more expensive product category such as cars, where you have the 'A', 'B', 'C', & 'D' segments defined.

Then how do you assess the price-pattern shown here, for cars?

Table 2.8: Prices of various models of cars and utility vehicles in Mumbai in 2003

Car Models and Prices			
Accent CRDi Diesel	758,065	Ambassador 2000 DSL	516,651
Accent GLS	639,660	Ambassador Nova Diesel	422,794
Accent GLX	703,281	Astra 1.6 Club (P)	934,416
Accent GTX - Tornado	767,465	Astra 1.6 GLi (P)	848,176
Accent GVS	598,658	Astra 1.6 GSi (P)	825,867
Accord VTi - AT	1,587,649	Astra 1.7 Club (D)	1,036,043
Accord VTi - MT	1,507,177	Astra 1.7 GSi (D)	878,264
Alto LXi	345,132	Astra 1.7 TD GLi (D)	940,198
Alto Vx	385,035	Baleno	832,010
Alto Vxi	406,679	Camry V1	1,870,580
Ambassador 1800 ISZ	477,494	Camry V3	1,923,468

(Contd.)

Table 2.8 (*Contd.*)

Car Models and Prices

Cielo	537,236	Maruti 800 EURO-2	225,420
Cielo (PS)	565,523	Matiz SA	411,000
Cielo CNG	576,454	Matiz SD	345,000
Cielo CNG (PS)	604,742	Matiz SG	363,000
City 1.5 (Exi) AT	921,907	Matiz SS	309,000
City 1.3 (Exi)	731,911	Mercedes C 180 -	2,330,922
City 1.3 (Lxi)	676,655	Mercedes C 180 - Classic	2,094,215
City 1.5 (Exi)	857,866	Mercedes C 200 CDI	2,379,537
City 1.5 (Exi) AT	921,907	Mercedes C 200 CDI	2,616,245
City 1.5 (Exi) S	893,437	Mercedes E 240 W211	3,963,120
City VTEC	960,536	Mercedes E 240 W211	3,963,120
Contessa Classic 1.8GLX	540,119	Mitsubishi Lancer GLX	957,777
Contessa Diesel 2.0 DL	551,529	(Diesel)	
Esteem AX EURO-2	669,870	Mitsubishi Lancer GLXi (Pet)	865,836
Esteem LX EURO-2	515,913	Mitsubishi Lancer SFX (I)	971,046
Esteem VXi	598,379	Mitsubishi Lancer SLX (D)	1,052,649
Gypsy King HT EURO-2	530,422	Mitsubishi Lancer SLX (I)	943,116
Gypsy King ST EURO-2	508,742	Mondeo Duratec - Petrol	1,629,548
Ikon 1.3 CLXi (E-Petrol)	534,094	Mondeo Duratorq - Diesel	1,759,012
Ikon 1.3 EXi (Endura-E-Petrol)	588,101	Nexia	630,712
Ikon 1.6 SXi (Rocam Petrol)	763,260	Nexia Deluxe	662,898
Ikon 1.6 ZXi (Rocam Petrol)	667,815	Octavia 1.9 TDi - Ambient	1,094,645
Ikon 1.8 SXi (Endura Diesel)	826,245	Octavia 1.9 TDi - Elegance	1,267,244
Ikon 1.8 ZXi (Endura Diesel)	738,195	Octavia 2.0 - Ambient	1,094,654
Indica DLE-V2	342,501	Octavia 2.0 - Elegance	1,327,264
Indica DL-V2	318,690	Omni (5-seater) EURO 2	247,548
Indica DLX-V2	420,193	Omni (8-seater) EURO 2	249,648
Indica LEi-V2	322,836	Omni Van XL EURO-2	249,649
Indica LXi-V2	401,407	Opel Corsa 1.4 GL	572,324
Indigo GLE	438,000	Opel Corsa 1.4 GLS	614,066
Indigo GLS	463,000	Opel Corsa 1.6 GSi	659,636
Indigo GLX	499,000	Opel Corsa 1.6 Royale	730,872
Indigo LS (Diesel)	484,000	Palio EL	361,801
Indigo LX (Diesel)	525,000	Palio EL (PS)	386,932
Mahindra Bolero GLX	538,700	Palio ELX (PS)	417,075
Mahindra Marshal DI	444,400	Palio GTX (PS)	518,580
Maruti 800 DX EURO 2	277,189	Palio GTX (SP/PS)	569,837
Maruti 800 DX Special		Palio Sport	440,193
EURO2	302,703	Qualis B4	579,429

(*Contd.*)

Table 2.8 (*Contd.*)

Car Models and Prices

Qualis B5	622,489	Siena 1.6 ELX	618,076
Qualis B6	655,059	Sonata 2.7 V6 H-Matic	1,613,543
Qualis C5	726,309	Sonata GLS	1,202,271
Qualis C8	802,109	Sonata Gold	1,322,189
Qualis D6	866,838.	Sumo - SE	459,194
Qualis FS/F5 10 ST	654,179	Sumo Deluxe (Non-metallic)	552,189
Qualis FS/F6 10 ST	686,805	Uno 1.2 Trend AC E-3	324,681
Qualis GS/G5 8 ST	762,927	Uno 1.2 Trend E-3	292,979
Qualis GS/G8 8 ST	837,634	Uno 1.7 Trend	339,100
Qualis GST Super	884,467	Uno 1.7 Trend AC	370,742
Qualis RS/E2 7 ST	890,011	Uno ELX (AC) E-3	371,235
Safari (4x2)	767,295	Uno ELX(AC/PS) - D	434,115
Safari (4x4)	843,361	Versa DX	553,978
Safari EX (4x2)	874,653	Versa DX 2	585,599
Safari EX (4x4)	972,272	Versa SDX	622,479
Santro Automatic	456,120	WagonR AX	518,087
Santro GS - 1.1	421,610	WagonR LX	357,625
Santro LE - 1.1	353,266	WagonR LXi	388,235
Santro LP - 1.1	369,240	WagonR VXi	410,549
Santro LS - 1.1	397,589	Zen AT	524,116
Scorpio Petrol	745,200	Zen D EURO-2	377,821
Scorpio Turbo 2.6	601,200	Zen LX EURO-2	368,157
Scorpio Turbo 2.6 DX	656,900	Zen Lxi EURO-2	397,734
Siena 1.2 EX	492,456	Zen Vxi EURO-2	429,659
Siena 1.6 EL	567,825		

Similar tables prepared for TV set models, washing machines, toilet soaps, readymade shirts, and a host of other categories would be just as extensive.

What these data reveal is a fundamental change that has taken place. Price certainly *will* be a partitioning variable between the *ends of a price spectrum*: no one will say that a Maruti 800 and a Mercedes 500 are 'competitors'; but this simplistic dismissal of the 'continuum-isation' of price is dangerous.

Consider the options available to someone who wishes to spend, say, Rs.500,000, assuming that the buyer is willing to consider models available within 15 per cent of this budget. Take a moment to actually check the models available in the price range between Rs.425,000 and Rs.575,000 in the table above. Would you have thought of them as 'competitors'?

Models in the price band we just looked at, are 'classified' by marketers as being in *different segments*. Would a prospective customer necessarily think so? Or would he see these as 'alternatives' within his budget, albeit with varying features and characteristics? (Of course there are issues such as that fact that some people who want a sedan will simply never look at a utility vehicle. But closeness of prices does some strange things: don't you know people who you would have never thought of as 'utility vehicle buyers' who have bought themselves say, a Tata Sumo or a Qualis?)

Let us take another category: toilet soaps. Now think of a fairly typical urban home. Perhaps there is a cake of Lifebuoy in the kids' bathroom. Maybe there is a cake of Dove, which is largely used for washing the face by the lady of the house. Perhaps there is also a cake of Cinthol, used by her young son. And in the cupboard, there are unopened cakes of other brands. Maybe a cake of Liril, picked up as a novelty; and, may be, a cake of Pears because grandma is coming over to stay and won't use anything else.

Now, just think of the price of a cake of each of the listed brands:

> Lifebuoy
> Dove
> Cinthol
> Liril
> Pears

Imagine yourself as the manager for each of these brands: Would the household, that we imagined a moment ago, be part of the target group for *all* these brands? Are they buyers of 'popular' soaps or 'premium' soaps? Why? Or, why not?

Awareness about repertoire buying and the fact that individuals buy brands across a fairly large price range is not new, but a lot of practitioners continue to see competition only in terms of similarly priced products. Far too often, this can be a mistake because when price gaps narrow, the competitive reference frame can change significantly.

2. DIMENSION: CHANGES IN PRODUCT CONFIGURATION

This involves the challenge from change in a fundamental characteristic or specific product attribute. Consider what happened in fabrics. By making quality polyester fabrics widely available, Vimal was literally able to 'polyester-ise' your wardrobe.

You could now get a shirt stitched which looked good, had a great design, and best of all, looked great even as you were wilting at the end of a hot, tiring day! Vimal changed the fabric market by bringing in a fundamentally new characteristic to fabrics: Drip-dry, no-ironing-needed, great looking fabric.

There are other changes, too, which have had a similar effect of creating new 'table stakes' in different categories.

Until the early 1990s in India, air conditioning in a car was a luxury and an 'option'. Today it is something that a car buyer thinks of as standard equipment. The same is true of car stereos, and soon will include, power steering, air bags and so on. Changes in product configuration can quickly make a brand outdated, if it cannot change fast enough to incorporate the new 'standards'.

The categories in which this has happened with the greatest speed are the technology categories such as computers and mobile phones. In the former, we have seen CD drives, graphics cards, improved sound capabilities and so on rapidly become basic features. The same is true in mobile handsets in which MMS capability, cameras, video recording and so on have moved from being cutting-edge to ordinary features.

3. Dimension: Distribution as a Competitive Advantage

Distribution was and still is clearly an important aspect of competitiveness for FMGC (Fast Moving Consumer Goods) brands. However, the fact is that it is also a critical success factor in other sectors and categories. Take banking as an example. It was not uncommon knowledge that the location of bank branches; specifically their proximity to one's place of residence or work, was an important criterion in choosing one's bank.

Here are the findings of a survey, which I had conducted in Mumbai a few years ago. The following table shows the answers to the question: How important are these factors in your choice of the bank in which to have an account?

Table 2.9 Importance of factors in selecting bank.

	Per cent saying Extremely Important
Should have a branch near home/office	77
Courteous staff	71
Quick service	71
Computerization	59
Extended hours of business	54
Reasonable charges for services	47
ATMs	36
Phone-banking facility	30

Source: Author's research

The branch network was something banks took as a 'given', one that they could do little about. This was especially so in the case of foreign banks, who faced restrictions on opening new branches. Clearly, people being more comfortable with a bank that had a branch close to their home or office was not a good sign, if you faced a severe handicap in terms of how large a branch network you could have. In addition, there was the enormous inertia that kept people from changing banks—going through the process of getting one's photograph taken, procuring the account opening form from a new bank, and so on was simply too tedious a process, for people to change their bank.

My team at Enterprise Advertising in the mid-1990s, working on Personal Banking for Standard Chartered Bank with Mr. Pradeep Mansukhani, changed that by creating the term 'Room Service' for the don't-come-to-us-we'll-come-to-you service of the bank. The concept was that a representative of the bank would come to your home or office, with the account opening forms, help you with all the formalities, including taking your photograph if necessary, and send you your ATM card, cheque book and so on to enable you to start operating your new account. Thanks to Phone Banking, ATMs and so on, it was actually possible to offer banking services conveniently, even without a branch network. The basic shift we created then has now become the norm in the industry.

4. DIMENSION: TECHNOLOGY

4.1: THE CHALLENGE OF ALTERNATIVE TECHNOLOGY

Before Titan watches were launched, most watches used 'mechanical' movements that required winding every 24 hours (there were also 'automatic' watches which did not need such winding, but 'mechanical' watches were the most common ones). Titan ushered in a fundamental change in watches by focusing on quartz watches. It altered the definition of what was seen as the technology standard in watches and completely eclipsed HMT in the consumers' mind. Its success with the new technology, and establishing leadership in that new technology, helped it to established market leadership in the category.

Recently, Citizen watches have been promoting watches with technology that eliminates the need to have batteries to power the movement. These watches with 'self-generating' power are termed eco-friendly. Think about whether Citizen, given the growing interest in eco-friendly practices, can bring around a similar re-definition and create the next 'standard of technology' in watches. If that is actually the intention of Citizen watches, does the current communication make you want to reject the current industry standard, and adopt the new one?

There are other categories where alternative technologies are creating different competitive spaces. Frost-free technology in refrigerators, for example, has created two sets of products: those that use the earlier technology, and those that use frost-free technology.

4.2: LEAPFROGGING THE 'G' IN GENERATIONS OF TECHNOLOGY

Yet another element that creates a flux in the market is the *successive generations of technology,* which may be competing with each other. In most categories, 'generations' of technology follow a chronological order with newer generations attempting to make older ones obsolescent. For example, the 'generations' of Pentium chips made by Intel have been improved products, intended to replace earlier versions (notwithstanding the fact that some users may continue to use computers with earlier chips!); or the 'generations' of automobile engines which have been designed to meet more stringent pollution control standards, such as Euro I and Euro II.

In many of these cases India lagged behind developed countries, and companies in India could observe the change taking place in the other markets and see 'what was coming'.

In the increasingly synchronous world of today however, companies do not have that advantage. We are literally leapfrogging over generations of technology that creates challenges of a completely different kind.

Take telephony for example. Here are the numbers on usage of landlines vs mobile connections. Ten years ago, there were 8 million phone lines in India. By the end of 2004, there were almost 90 million connections, 47 million of them mobile phone connections.

What do you think should be Mahanagar Telephone Nigam Limited (MTNL)'s response? Do they focus on their bread and butter business—that is, landlines? How do they compete with the mobile phone service providers?

Or consider calculators. What future do they have with the calculation functionality built into mobile phone handsets, PDAs and other devices?

Consider what happened to pagers. Internationally, there was a gap of several years between the availability and adoption of pagers and later on, cell phones. Pager services, therefore, went through a classic Product Life Cycle, before cell phone technology arrived. In the Indian market however, the time-gap between the two was minimal. As a consequence, the pager business was more or less stillborn. As India rapidly catches up with the world in all categories, many brands are going to find themselves having to compete in these generation-transition situations.

While it may not appear as if this is likely to happen in your business immediately, step back for a moment, and think.

- What is the continuing reduction in the cost of scanners going to do to you, if you are marketing a brand of photocopier?
- With email and jpeg files, broadband connections and larger storage capacity for email accounts, is the fax machine redundant, living on borrowed time?
- If mobile phones take-off, what is the future for camera makers in India? For makers of photo film? For *processors* of camera film? Already, internationally there are more mobile phones with cameras being sold than digital cameras. Kodak has learnt to 'sleep with the enemy' as camera phones become more common, and offers a service where you can take the picture on your cell phone and yet print it out on Kodak paper!

Summing Up

This chapter was intended to help you start off your process of creating strong brands by considering the changing bases of competition, and identifying the forces of change likely to affect your brand. Here are the key points made in this chapter.

- *It was the arrival of a cost-efficient medium that had an all-India reach, that allowed many brands to build the kind of high awareness and trial, which was fundamental to converting them from regional players to major national brands. At the other end of the media spectrum too, there are changes taking place, which have opened up markets for specialized product categories with more focused target groups. For example, publications such as Autocar and Motoring have enabled makers of vehicles, auto parts, and accessories to reach individuals with a particular interest in cars and motorbikes.*
- *Business magazines and TV channels have provided an avenue for advertising financial products, office equipment, high-end personal products, telecom products and services, and more.*

  Other specialized media such as Interiors and Architectural Digest have provided a means of reaching people in the building, construction, design and furniture industries.
- *With changes in lifestyles and technological innovations, and growing competition, one needs to be conscious of threats which are coming from outside category—defined sets of products and brands as consumers 'cross over' categories as defined in the past.*
- *We also noted that it is important to realise that even as the simple divisions between categories are breaking down, the 'constellation of competition' is itself being redefined by other changes. Some of these developments have the effect of creating greater aggregates of competition. In other cases, we are seeing the fragmentation of categories into sub-groups.*

Finally we looked at the key dimensions of competition within categories, noting that the major ones are:

- ○ *The reduction in price gaps creating price spectra where earlier there were 'price points'*
- ○ *How changes in some basic characteristic or feature of a product creates competitive change*
- ○ *We saw the challenge of overcoming a distribution advantage competition might have*
- ○ *Finally, we looked at how technological changes can affect and redefine the competitive landscape*

The Action Point formats given below will help you to assess the changing nature of the factors affecting your brand, and the likely competitive challenges it will face.

We need to analyse changes at two levels. First, study the changes that impact the *overall product category.* These affect an entire category and are usually changes in social norms, people's expectations, lifestyle and habit, etc.

Now imagine that we represent a small co-operative bank—ABC Co-operative Bank—and consider the changes affecting banking services, especially in four areas:

1. **Usage Characteristics:** We may say that our current customers largely use the bank accounts only for salary deposits, or to issue cheques and withdraw cash for household expenses. However, the change we observe across customers of all banks is that they are becoming more interested in investments, and in ensuring that their money grows. Therefore they are now more interested in shares, mutual funds, and the like. The competitive implication of this is that *all banks will face competition from other financial service companies.* This will encourage depositors to take 'idle' money out of savings accounts and make investments. Banks, in turn, will lose the low-cost money made available to them (so far possible due to the very low interest rate paid on customers' money in their savings accounts).

2. Next, let us look at the way customers are **Classifying Products** and the way they see **Key Product Characteristics:** Currently, banks are seen as different from—or similar to—each other, based on their ownership. Most people classify banks into four main types: PSU (public sector unit) banks, Indian private banks, Co-operative banks and MNC (multinational corporation) banks.

    This is changing because differences amongst them are becoming less and less. MNC banks are becoming friendlier, and Indian banks are offering the latest technology. As a result, a bank will face competition from all types of banks, at an individual bank brand level.

3. In terms of **Product Characteristics,** the biggest change is that, instead of banking at branches, it is happening via phone banking, Internet banking and ATMs. This 'off-branch' banking may become the critical factor in years to come.

4. Finally when we consider **Service, Performance and Delivery Characteristics**, we see that customers are expecting *all services at one place*—including investing in Mutual Funds, paying taxes, buying foreign exchange, etc. We—as a bank—are not yet ready to offer the same, at all branches. This has serious implications, since our bank will now be compared to even investment (service) companies. Also, we do not know how our image compares with this new class of 'competitors'.

We now sum up the above example of assessment of Category-level changes: you must do this as the first step of the planning process, for your product or service category.

Assessment of Category-Level Changes
Example: Banks

Dimension	Assessment of your brand	Changes likely to affect it	Competitive implications
Key Usage Characteristics	Basic deposit of salaries, other income and withdrawal or issue of cheques for expenses	Greater interest in investments including shares, mutual funds, etc.	- Competition from 'Investment advisory' companies - Less 'idle' funds in savings accounts: impact on cost of funds
Basis of Product Classification by Customers	Banks are seen as different or similar based on ownership: PSU banks, Indian private banks, Co-operative banks and MNC banks	MNC banks becoming more 'approachable' PSU banks also becoming more service oriented	Banks likely to compete as individual brands, rather than being 'clubbed' in earlier groups

(Contd.)

(Contd.)

Dimension	Assessment of your brand	Changes likely to affect it	Competitive implications
Key Product Characteristics	Most of our customers come to the branches to get services	Increased 'off-branch' banking reducing perceived differences across these categories	Quality of off-branch service may become critical differentiator
Service/Performance/Delivery Characteristics	'All services at one place' becoming common consumer choice. We however, do not have any investment advisory services at most branches. Customers have to come to the Head office for these services.	Brings in comparison with investment services	Non-banking companies such as Kotak are entering the competitive space – What is our image among this competitive set?

Second, you need to look at changes occurring *within the category, at a brand level.* For the same, let us continue with our example of the co-operative bank:

The first change we must consider is the one occurring in the **Price Spectrum.** Here, we see that many banks have started charging extra for extra services. With the fall in interest rates we are charging on loans, we are now earning less. Therefore we, too, will have to cut costs and start charging our customers for those extra services. This will change the perception about the price of banking services; since most services—such as additional cheque-books or phone banking services—are currently given free of cost. This will also raise a question in the customers' minds, about the value they are getting for the fee they are paying.

We, the bank, will have to inform our customers of all details regarding new charges: how frequently they will be charged, etc. If we do not spell out these charges, it may bring about consumer dissatisfaction. In the past, customers partaking of banking services have felt cheated on discovering 'extra' charges (stated only in the fine print of some bank literature). Customers may also feel dissatisfied at having to now pay for what was free all these years. The challenge, then, is to give them improved services so as to make them feel that the extra charges are justified.

Next area to think about is that of **Changes In Product Characteristics:** Features and services—credit card, debit cards, depository accounts, wide network of ATMs, etc.—are seen by customers as basic offerings from banks. They are table stakes in the new competitive situation. Secondly, while MNC banks have always been perceived as having a lead in the technology of banking; new, private Indian banks like HDFC and ICICI are believed to offer technology as good as—if not better than—that offered by MNC banks. Even PSU banks are catching up—offering credit cards, ATMs and the like.

Both MNC and PSU banks are also trying to correct their customer-*unfriendly* image, by making their services more customer-friendly and warm.

The question arises: Is our brand getting stuck somewhere in the middle, in danger of losing the edge of being the 'best of both worlds' (good technology and warm service)?

Third area to examine is the **Changes In The Distribution System.** In banking, the biggest change in distribution is emergence of 'off-branch' service capability, through ATMs, phone banking, Internet banking and via mobile phone. We have a large branch network, but only a limited number of ATMs. This will be unsatisfactory for many customers who wish to carry out 'off-branch' banking transactions, and at a time convenient to them. Not having enough ATMs could become a severe handicap in this case. The implication is that even banks with very few branches—maybe only one or two in a city—can now target and grab a share of our customers by offering them high quality off-branch services.

Finally we must consider **Changes In Technology.** Changes in distribution and the change in technology are related. While many banks have computerised their baking 100 per cent, we do not have it; nor do we offer Internet banking and banking services on mobile phones. We are thus losing out in the technology game. With consumers using computers and mobile phones in their day-to-day life and for a variety of services, phone banking, Internet banking and banking services on mobile phones are fast becoming minimum expectations. This may lead to some customers closing their account with us, and moving on to another bank.

The biggest threat to us is that even those who retain their account in our bank may simultaneously open another one in a more technologically advanced bank. It is possible that these people have *two* bank accounts; with customers doing a major part of their banking through the other bank/account that offers technologically superior facilities.

This analysis, which is at the inter-bank level *within the category*, can be summarised as:

**Assessment of Changes within the category:
Example – ABC Co-operative Bank**

Dimension	Assessment of your brand	Changes likely to affect it	Competitive implications
Changes in Price Spectrum	Other banks are charging for extra services. We will also have to start charging for such services	Not clearly spelling out charges can cause consumer dissatisfaction.	Our customers may get angry at paying for things they have got free all these years
Changes in Product Characteristics	Inclusion of Credit card, Depository account, ATMs, etc. becoming table stakes	MNC banks have had perceived lead in the technology of banking. PSUs also catching up. Both also trying to make their service more customer friendly and warm	Is our brand losing its edge as the 'best of both worlds' (good technology and warm service)?
Changes in Distribution System	We have a large branch network, but a limited number of ATMs	More and more banking customers doing 'off-branch' transactions. Not having ATMs could become a severe handicap	Banks with even very few branches can grab share from us through offering
Changes in Technology	We do not have 100 per cent computerisation; nor have a platform to deliver Internet banking and banking services on mobiles	Phone banking, Internet banking and banking services on mobiles are becoming minimum expectations	It is likely that people will have two bank accounts, with the customer doing a major part of their banking through another account which offers such facilities

Chapter 2: Action Point-1
Assessment of Category-level Changes

Dimension	Assessment of Your Brand	Changes Likely to Affect IT	Competitive Implications
Key Usage Characteristics			
Basis of Product Classification by Customers			
Key Product Characteristics			
Service/ Performance/ Delivery Characteristics			

Chapter 2: Action Point-2
Assessment of Changes within the Category

Dimension	Assessment of Your Brand	Changes Likely to Affect IT	Competitive Implications
Changes in Price Spectrum			
Changes in Product Characteristics			
Changes in Distribution System			
Changes in Technology			

Communication in Context

The Marketing Drivers of Brands

Overview

When people go to Paris, they don't want to miss seeing the Eiffel Tower, and when they visit India they want to visit the Taj Mahal.

If you are in the tourism business, you need to know what it is about a particular place that turns people on.

They made a film starring Amitabh Bachchan in which they changed his voice. (It is the equivalent of making a Madhubala film, throughout which she is filmed in a burkha.) Is it any wonder the film flopped?

If you want to make successful films, it is important to know the importance of Amitabh's voice or Madhubala's smile, in getting people to watch a film.

The point is, you must capitalize on what works best for your brand. In fact, not just what works for your brand, but what actually drives the people who choose it in preference over other brands.

In this chapter we will look at the way different factors can be the drivers for brands, and look at examples of brands that have capitalized on different drivers.

Imagine for a moment that you put the following question to various people associated with Madhuri Dixit (or Rani Mukherjee, or whoever is *your* favourite actress): *What is the secret of her attractiveness?*

If you were speaking to the jeweller who had created the adornments for Madhuri Dixit, chances are, he will tell you that it was the ornaments he designed for her which made her look gorgeous.

Of course, if you spoke to her make-up man, he'd tell you how it was the way he highlighted her smile that made all the difference.

And if you spoke to her dress designer, she would say...well, you get the idea.

The point is that each of these statements is true. It is equally true that each of these statements does not tell the full story. Almost by definition, each element of the *total brand offer* is important; but equally true is the fact that each brand must discover—and focus on, the particular element that yields the maximum benefit per rupee spent. Let me take some examples from Indian films that may illustrate the concept more dramatically.

Jeetendra, from the very first time that he began to jump around in *Farz*, wearing white shoes and trousers, must have realized that *his* strength—in what I have called '**the 4-D's' of Indian cinema**'—was Dancing.

In a momentary detour, let us consider these 4-D's of Indian films.

Dancing—the first D: The ability to shake a leg (or the entire body, if you will!), has always been a critical aspect of the popularity of film stars, given the escapist nature of most Indian films. Exponents have created several 'owned' styles. We have seen the range from the 'minimalistic moves of Bhagwan in *Albela*' to the syncopated moves of Amitabh Bachchan in a *Mr. Natwarlal*. We have seen the range from the ballet-like grace of a Hritik Roshan to the break-dance moves of a Prabhudeva. We have seen the gamut of moves from the frenzied actions of a Rishi Kapoor to the uncopiable energy of Shammi Kapoor. The moves are the magic.

Dramatics—the second D: In Indian films, it is the ability to engage the emotions of the viewers and get them to feel a shared anger at injustice and the pathos of a betrayed love. It is the 'D' that has led to dialogues, which have become part of the language and continue to stir emotions over the years. (Example: Shashi Kapoor's, '*Mere paas maa hai*' 'response in *Deewar*. Translation: 'I have mother with me').

Seen in the powerful emotional impact of Dilip Kumar's performances from *Madhumati, Aadmi, Ram aur Shyam* to *Shakti* to *Mashaal*. Displayed by Naseeruddin Shah in *Sparsh, Pestonji* and many other films. By Amitabh Bachchan in films like *Deewar* and *Zanjeer* and *Baghbaan*. Visible in Sanjeev Kumar's portrayals in *Anubhav, Khilona, Koshish* and *Angoor*. And in the roles Rajesh Khanna has played in *Anand, Aradhana, Ittefaq, Amar Prem* and *Khamoshi*.

Dashing Style—the third D: This variable depends on making *the sizzle so appealing, that you don't even notice whether there was a steak!* This is the driver that determined the success of a Dev Anand, of a Shashi Kapoor, or internationally, of a Gregory Peck. You are so charmed by the actor that style *becomes* the substance!

Doofus-Appeal—the fourth D: It is the appeal of a lost puppy. The appeal of someone who looks so lost and naïve that you begin to worry about how he will look after himself. The appeal stems from the basic assumption that if people think you are a simpleton and look as if you can't take care of yourself, then someone *else* will think *they* should take care of you!

It's not as silly as it sounds, after all, Dharmendra, Amol Palekar, Guru Dutt (to an extent), and above all, Raj Kapoor gained huge fan-followings on this basis. *Perhaps, inside every woman there is a care-giver who seeks a 'victim' of life, whom she can protect from the hostile world!*

The point of this detour was not to initiate a discussion on Indian films. It was intended to highlight the fact that there are several different potential bases to develop brand preferences, but that you should commit to which one will be your most important competitive driver.

This is a simple guideline, and everyone agrees with it at a conceptual level. Unfortunately, the temptation to extend appeal by looking at more than one aspect is an all too common expression of intellectual laziness and lack of operational focus. To bring this into sharper focus, think of whether Dilip Kumar ever attempted to 'compete' on the 'dancing' dimension. Or whether Jeetendra attempted to establish his credentials in the dramatic ability area, at the cost of ignoring his dancing ability. Dev Anand leveraged his sophisticated-romantic image—he never played a rural bumpkin. (Given the 'hero can do anything' omnipotence of Indian stars, of course they did bits of everything, but you must *understand what was the driver!*)

The simple lesson to be drawn from these examples is that brands should *focus on, and leverage their strengths,* rather than attempt to become that which they are not; that a brand must choose and then concentrate its efforts on one dimension. (This is not to say that the others are irrelevant—tactically, you may look at other dimensions, as a Dilip Kumar may have danced in a film or two—but that the owners of the brand are clear *which their strength area is*).

Let us consider some of the key dimensions available, and the manner in which brands have leveraged these as drivers.

This is actually the first step in planning advertising, where the marketers and their communications partners need to look at potential brand drivers, and identify the one they will focus on.

(*Note of caution:* In an age where tangibles are seen as only providing parity, the previous statements might seem like a suggestion for a return to an era of thinking which has gone by. Let me clarify. It is true that intangibles create brand differentials and preferences that last even when a brand loses its edge on tangible factors; however there is a danger of taking this too far. Because it is also true that brands cannot be built out of nothing. I suspect that the virtual elimination of tangibles from thinking, has often led to the launch of brands which have nothing tangible to offer by way of a strength, by marketers, who then expect too much from communication to create a difference. In my view, while intangibles are what excite the emotions and senses, there has to be something tangible underlying it. Think of this in the context of ordering a sizzler at a restaurant: yes, it is the 'intangible' aromas and the sound of the sizzle which gets the mouth watering—but sooner or later you need something to bite into!)

Brand Drivers are the tangible foundations on which the intangibles can be built.

BRAND DRIVER 1: CHOICE OF TARGET SEGMENT

One of the first choices a brand must make is: Which consumer segment do I really want to cater to? It is not as easy a question to answer as may appear at first consideration, because *it implies giving up some prospect groups to focus on a particular one*. Benetton focuses on young people, for its T-Shirts, and *chooses* to forgo the golf-club crowd. On the other hand, Lacoste focuses on the 30+ 'lounge sportsman' and accepts that it is ignoring the teenyboppers.

Here are some examples of other brands, which have chosen to leverage their association with a specific target group.

MTV: This is an example of a brand, which in a fundamental way, *created* a psychographic segment. Targeting the youth of America through its mix of music and lifestyle programming, it has created a world to which the youth aspire to belong, and see as their sanctum from the boring world of the adult establishment.

The brand has developed a crazy, wild, idiosyncratic style for its 'communication', and a brand lexicon which defines the language, clothing and tastes of the youth segment. It is more than a brand that targets youth; it is the very forum for their expressions and aspirations. No wonder it has acquired the iconic status it commands: After all, how many brands have an entire generation named after them?!

MTV is so clear about what it stands for, that even its communication to business prospects (its invitations, mailers, etc.) carry the same spirit of wildness. It is this unwavering, undeniable focus on a particular target group that makes MTV the image-leader as a youth-brand.

The MTV poster (Figure 3.1) is a good example of its idiosyncratic, irreverent style of communication.

Elle 18: Another brand, which has steadfastly focused on the younger, 'I'm-just-learning-to-use-make-up-regularly' opportunity.

Many of the other brands in cosmetics could or even should have done this, as they saw the changing patterns in fashion and grooming. Yet they did not. Elle 18 did. And it leveraged its association with a closely-defined

**Figure 3.1: Press advertisement: MTV appeals to youth
with its wacky style**

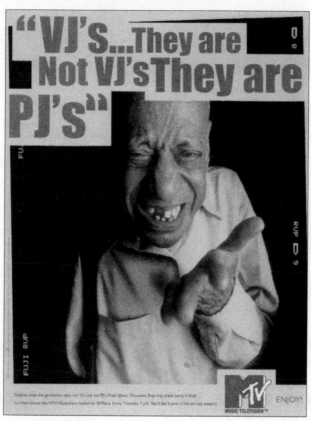

prospect group, through its advertising, the product nomenclature, and even promotions (for example, a promotion in which the participant had to create a shade which would then be 'named' after her.).

It is also important to understand that it required a new brand to adopt this very sharp focus. If it had been attempted under the umbrella of an *existing brand* such as Lakme, the result would probably be more of a loss of Lakme's focus on the adult woman, rather than a capitalization on the opportunity represented by the younger target segment.

The questions to ask yourself to identify whether you should make the target group the driver for your brand are:

- ○ Are there sharply defined, distinct target segments that are being targeted by major brands in our category?
- ○ Are there other distinct target segments, which my brand can focus on?

Figure 3.2: Press advertisement: Elle 18, showing the clear focus in a young, trendy target customer

○ What inputs/support can we employ to focus uniquely on this target segment?

BRAND DRIVER 2: THE PRODUCT OR SERVICE

In our increasingly competitive scenario, it may seem difficult for a brand to achieve and maintain product and service differentials. However, this is a very important driver if it can be developed. In fact, if you *do* have a product or service driver, you need to try and figure out how you can own it, even though you know competition will try to imitate or replicate this factor.

Here are some examples of brands, which have product or service drivers, underlying all the intangibles they are associated with.

Moov: For decades, Iodex was the 'first aid' a person reached for, to gain relief from a hurting ankle or leg or a muscular ache. However, it was more associated with severe muscular pain, such as sprains. Moov created a very simple but powerful driver based on developing two important product differences:

(a) it was a white/clear cream unlike the dark ointment of Iodex, and
(b) it came in a tube.

(Of course, it also leveraged the fact that backaches occur more commonly than sprains, and require application of a larger quantity of cream over a larger area, to build consumption volume for the brand.)

Dettol: It is a safe bet that you would be able to tell the smell of Dettol with your eyes closed. Moreover, when you apply Dettol liquid on a cut or wound, there is a reassuring tingling sensation, which tells you it's begun to work. These product characteristics are a key aspect of Dettol's equity.

Savlon antiseptic on the other hand, which does *not* have the same burning sensation, has very often been seen by consumers, as 'ineffective' compared to Dettol. Savlon has attempted in communication, to make a virtue of this absence of a burning sensation. But while this absence of burning/tingling is certainly a major advantage in say, a post-operative application (where the irritation caused by Dettol would be unbearable), it is unable to offer the 'tingling proof of performance' which Dettol provides, in the case of minor cuts and wounds. Indeed it is such an intrinsic part of Dettol's equity, that a Dettol line extension without the smell or tingling sensation is likely to be seen as ineffective or worse, 'spurious'.

Nordstorm: The no-questions-asked return policy of Nordstrom as the basis of its strong equity has been written about too often to need repetition. Suffice it to say that the brand stands for commitment to customer satisfaction to an extent, which any retailer brand would envy. And it has been built on a tangible aspect of service.

Apple computer: The fundamental *tangible, product* differences between Apple computers and the 'grey boxes', have been a cornerstone of the brand since it was launched. The brand decided at the outset, that it was going to be distinctive and noticeably so, in many fundamental ways.

- The very design of Apple computers, iPods and other products is based on a brilliant fusion of form and function
- The concept of its software is based on using the computer *intuitively*
- And it seems to *anticipate* consumer needs and design products and services to cater to them

From the original Macintosh to the iBook to the iPod to iTunes to the design of their keyboards and mouse to a host of other initiatives, this philosophy is evident in everything that makes an Apple an Apple. In fact today, Apple is not only setting the direction in computer design, it is doing so in consumer electronics in audio and video products, which challenges consumer product companies. Nathan Myhrvold, former chief of Microsoft Research, in talking about this development is quoted in *Fortune* (issue dated February 21, 2005). He says, 'Once audio and visual experiences become a combined hardware-software-network thing, the consumer electronics guys are fish out of water'

Dove: It looks like a bar of soap, and users use it the way they would use soap. And retailers also stock it next to soaps. Yet the communication tells us, 'Dove is not a soap, it is 1/4th moisturizing cream.' This is the kind of product differential, which can be a major driver for a brand.

Figure 3.3: Press advertisement: Dove tells you it is not quite a soap

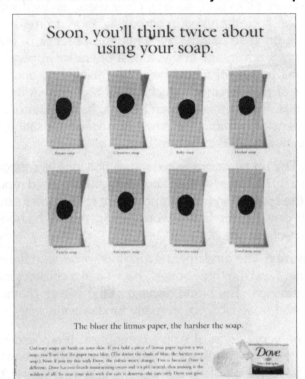

Sony: Although it is being challenged on its audio 'home turf' by Apple, has also made the product a key driver of the brand and pushed technology to deliver superior offerings in the face of dozens of competitors. This has been evident from the Trinitron tube to the Walkman, to the Sony PlayStation. It has helped them set the standard for the category such as the Trinitron tube, created products which became so popular that they became the generic term for the entire category such as 'Walkman' (for personal stereos), and helped them build category leaders like the Sony PlayStation, even in categories they entered late, and which had dominant brands (such as Nintendo).

And even the exceptional *aspirational and 'intangible' appeal* of a Rolls Royce is built on the product reality of the wood used for the panels, the leather used for the upholstery, and the so on.

The questions to ask yourself to identify whether you should make the Product or Service the driver for your brand are:

- What are the differentiators we will commit to in terms of the product or service?
- Do we have patents/intellectual focus/R&D practices and so on to maintain these differentiators?
- What are the processes and systems we will adopt to ensure that we retain the power of this driver?
- How easily can competitors copy our product or service? How can we make it more difficult for them to copy us?

BRAND DRIVER 3: PRICE

Most often, price is not used as a long-term driver for a brand. Rather, it is used as either a market entry strategy ('Maximum Retail Price Rs.100. Introductory offer: Rs.15 off!'), or as a tactical promotional tool. But that is not necessarily so; it is also possible to make price a fundamental aspect of the brand's strategy.

Here are examples of brands, which have used price as the driver for the brand.

Nirma: This is probably the best-known case, in recent times, of a brand that used price as a driver. At a time when Surf was priced at over Rs.20/Kg, and other brands such as Point, and Key were available around Rs.15/Kg, Nirma was launched at almost a third of the price of Surf. It changed the very structure of the washing products market, led to an explosion in the 'powder' category, and eventually compelled Hindustan Lever to launch Wheel around the new price-point which had been created.

Videocon and Akai: First Videocon, and later Akai, helped to make TVs the most commonly owned consumer durable (after fans) in Indian homes by making them available at affordable prices. Videocon has also done the same for washing machines.

Peter England: This brand of readymade garments became a huge success in just a few months when it was launched at prices 'from Rs.395' in a market in which well-made, widely advertised, national brands were perceived to be priced at Rs.500 plus.

indiOne Hotels: I was involved very closely with The Taj Group of hotels in the launch of an entirely new kind of hotel with room tariffs under Rs.1000 per night (before taxes.) But with facilities that one associates with much higher tariffs. Such as meeting rooms, gym facilities, a cyber cafe on the premises, as well as wireless Internet connectivity in the public areas as well as individual rooms, TFT screen colour television, in-room tea and coffee maker, etc.

Figure 3.4: Press advertisement: The first indiOne hotel

This service-bundle, which is termed Smart Basics™ reflects the way that people live and work today; where the operative principles are: independence, self-reliance and value for time. These are visible in the way people now use email instead of letters, and use mobile phones, conference calls and video-conferences instead of travelling to get things done quickly and efficiently. In the same way, people use ATMs and phone banking services at times that suit them, rather than go to a bank branch at hours set by others.

This is a useful place to reiterate the way in which price should be used as a driver: it is not the use of lower price alone—that is the way which leads towards commodification. Indeed, categories such as moulded luggage fell into this trap and were commoditised.

Rather, the idea is to *use price as an intrinsic element of creating new Price-Performance Points,* and thereby build differentiated brands.

Often, when we think of brands which use price as a driver, we think only about low-priced brands. But it is not so. Price can also be used as a driver at the other end of the spectrum. Joy perfume, for many years, used the tagline, 'The most expensive perfume in the world. Several brands of watches in India recently have celebrated their high prices as evidence of their value as precision instruments and objects of desire. The Maybach from Daimler Chrysler is almost never mentioned without its stratospheric price being mentioned in the same breath.

Here are a few other ways in which Price is used by some brands:

Leading edge component Pricing: It is well known that for a brand like Kodak, whose primary business was photographic film, it made eminent sense to sell *cameras at a low price* to create opportunities for the sale of film.

However, the fly in the ointment in the strategy is that, having bought a low-priced Kodak camera, the consumer is free to then go out and buy Fuji film! Such a strategy however, can work if a 'one-size-does-*not*-fit-all' product is devised; as in the case of Gillette, where the only cartridge that fits a Gillette razor, is a Gillette cartridge.

Unbundled Pricing: In some categories, it is common to sell only the 'basic product', leaving the buyer to buy the other parts piecemeal.

In the case of bicycles, for instance, you can buy the basic frame and wheels of say an Atlas cycle; and then 'assemble' the rest of your bike by choosing, separately, the seat, bell, carrier, stand, lock, rear-view mirror and headlamp. This allows the bicycle manufacturer to sell the basic product at what appears to be a more reasonable price, and lets the retailer make more money on the accessories. Of course, in the premium models of bicycles, most of the parts are 'coordinated', and the entire ensemble is sold as one package.

Bundled Pricing: This is another strategy which operates in the opposite direction, and is quite common in some categories; for instance, in furniture. The very notion of 'coordination' is so important in this category, that it allows a brand like 'The Living Room' in Mumbai, to put together bundled-pricing combinations of furniture. Often, these bundles are created around a unifying thought such as 'Bedroom Package' or 'Living and Dining Room Set'

However, it is important for managers of a brand to be aware of the exact role the price is playing in their strategy. This is because price is often not recognized for its strategic value.

The most common factor which works against retaining price as a driver is the 'lure of volume', which high-priced brands fall prey to, or the 'lure of prestige', which low-priced brands face. This is created by the fundamental inverse relationship between price and volume as shown below.

Figure 3.5: The inverse relationship between volume and prestige/price

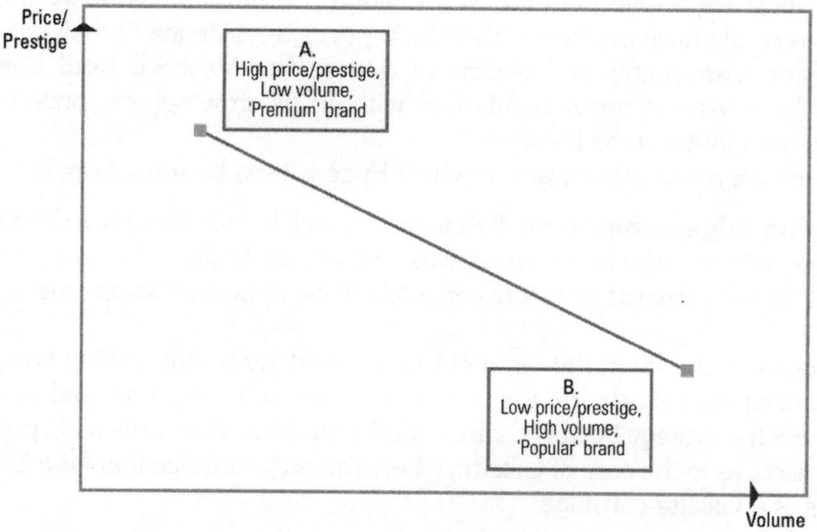

Brand custodians often adopt one of two strategies in such situations, both aimed at turning the brands into exactly *what they are not*.

One, brand B might increase price to gain more prestige and margins (Or, A may reduce price to gain volume).

Two, the brands might introduce line extensions to create offerings at a different price point.

Both approaches, most often, fail. The associations evoked by the low-price brand are usually not compatible with a higher-priced prestigious offering. Further, the move serves to point out the limitations of the low-priced original. Consider for instance the limited success achieved by the Maruti brand in premium cars. Similarly, Videocon has not been as successful with premium TV sets.

On the other hand, the introduction of a lower-priced version of a premium brand makes it more accessible, and reduces the exclusivity associated with the brand. Onida has sought to avoid this by launching the 'Igo' brand at a lower price point to seek larger volumes, while avoiding a negative impact on the Onida image.

The reason these strategies usually don't work is that, in both cases, these moves *undermine the very basis of the success of the brand.*

And before anyone suggests that price can only be used as a tactical tool and not as a strategic element, it is worth remembering that the basic mission of Wal-Mart, the biggest company in the world with sales of over US$ 250 billion, is: 'To lower the world's cost of living.' That's why, as reported by *Fortune* magazine, its store managers are given the power to lower prices, but not to raise them.

The important thing is not to look at price in isolation, whether at the low or high-end, but rather to *redefine the Price-performance point, and thereby create a driver for the brand.*

The following figure illustrates the point.

Figure 3.6: Redefining the Price-Performance point

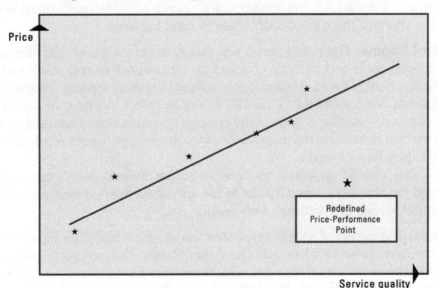

The questions to ask yourself in order to identify whether you should make 'Pricing' the driver for your brand are:

  ○ What do we represent: a different price point or a different Price-Performance Point?

  ○ What would happen to our consumers (would we lose them? would they accept it?) if we increased the price? What if we reduced it?

BRAND DRIVER 4: DISTRIBUTION

At one level, brand distribution is clearly an issue of *necessity*—to make it possible for consumers to access the product or service. But there are certain cases where brands have used distribution in a far more important sense, and used it as a brand driver.

Banking: As we saw earlier, among the most important criteria based on which customers chose a particular bank, was whether it had a branch near their home or place of work. We also saw that the Personal Banking group at Standard Chartered Bank (SCB) followed an innovative approach to tackle this issue: since they couldn't increase the number of branches, according to RBI rules, could they make it easier for customers to open an account with them by reversing the process? Instead of the consumer coming to the bank, a bank representative went to the customer, to facilitate opening the account. SCB's 'Room Service' offer changed the rules of the banking game, soon became a standard for the industry, and, along with Phone Banking and ATMs, changed the role of distribution in retail banking.

Petrol Pumps: The petrol pump was simply the place where you filled up your petrol tank, and perhaps checked the air pressure of your car's tyres. Now, it is turning into a retailing point, offering a host of services. Hindustan Petroleum has created the 'Club HP' brand to reflect this new view of the petrol pump—another change in the concept of distribution. There are news reports that Reliance is planning major innovations in the petrol retail outlets they expect to soon open.

  HP has created an entire '*Achcha lagta hai*' ('Feels good') campaign around the new experience thanks to the special services offered under the Club HP service of Hindustan Petroleum.

Paints: The notion of advice and service has also been added to expand the 'distribution' network of brands like Asian Paints. The company offers a service wherein a householder can call a painting expert to assess the painting needs and suggest options. By creating a 'take the mountain to Mohammed' approach, as in the case of SCB, Asian Paints is effectively extending its distribution system right up to the consumers' doorstep.

Other examples are abundant. No doubt you can come up with many, but here are a few to get you thinking:

- o The role of 'home delivery' that is now being extended even by cinema theatres like Fame Adlabs.
- o The role of the Internet in building brands such as Amazon.
- o The role of creating 'cafes-in-a-shop' in taking a brand like Barista inside shopping complexes and bookstores, in locations where a full-fledged café may not have been feasible or financially viable.

All these are examples of the way brands can use distribution as a key driver.

The questions to ask yourself to identify whether you should make Distribution the driver for your brand are:

- o Are there ways in which consumers access the product/service which are limiting my brand?
- o Can we do anything to make this access a basis for preference for our brand?
- o Can we 'protect' these mechanisms from being copied easily?

Think carefully about your brand and carry out a Brand Driver Analysis:

Is there a potential driver you are not harnessing? Consider the following example, which explores alternative Target Groups as drivers for a brand of credit cards. It is left to the reader to carry out a similar assessment by thinking about the product or service, the pricing and other potential drivers for his or her brand. Some brands are suggested for the exercise.

The format given in the Action Point can be used to carry out the analysis for your brands.

Sample: Brand Driver Analysis

As an example for Brand Driver Analysis, let us consider a hypothetical brand of credit cards. The assumption made in this sample analysis is that it is the *Target Group,* which is the Brand Driver for credit cards. We may begin with the thought that the *Current* view of the people being targeted by credit cards is 'salaried & business white-collar workers in SEC A'. We note this in the Brand Driver Analysis format.

Next, *Assess* this Current view. We may conclude that such a general definition of Target Group was sufficient in the days when only one or two brands of credit cards were available; but in today's more competitive environment, where there are several such brands available, it is necessary to target a more specific group in order to differentiate our brand. So we conclude that the current Target Group definition is *diffused and does not provide any focus for brand activities.*

Yet, that is not enough. We need to think about which group or groups can represent a big, future opportunity for our brand. Looking at the potential and fact that there is a big growth of professionals foraying into management, we may say that one segment which could offer a big market could be 'Tomorrow's Executive' i.e. today's student of management/professional course. And, what is the Assessment that leads us to believe this? It is the fact that currently there is *no credit card designed specifically for students.* Potentially this is a very large group, and worth considering in greater detail.

Not stopping at the first idea, let us think of at least one more potentially large target group for our credit card. We may then arrive at the fact that more and more women are joining the workforce. Which means, they have independent incomes, and discretionary spending. This would clearly offer an opportunity to create a differentiated, and unique brand—specifically designed for working women. Evidently, the credit card would need to have relevant affiliations for the services it offers. For example, it could tie-up with Lakme beauty salons (for special services to card-holders), or with the department of Gynaecology in hospitals (for healthcare services). Table 3.1 offers a summary of this analysis.

Table 3.1: Format for analyzing the drivers of a brand and sample analysis done for credit cards

	Target Group	*Product or Service*	*Pricing*	*Distribution*
Product/ Brand Current	Credit Card The universe of salaried & business white-collar workers in SEC A.	McDonalds	Provogue shirts	Café Coffee Day
Brand Driver Assessment	Diffused. Does not provide any focus for brand activities.			
Potential Driver Approach 1	Tomorrow's executive i.e. today's student of management or a professional course.			
Brand Driver Assessment	High leverage possible. No current card designed for students.			

(Contd.)

Table 3.1 (*Contd.*)

		Target Group	Product or Service	Pricing	Distribution
		Potentially very large group.			
Potential Driver Approach 2		Working women.			
Brand Driver Assessment		Opportunity to build differentiation through dedicated-affiliated services. Need to estimate size of segment.			

Summing Up

The main take-out of this chapter is intended to be that each element of the total brand offer is important; but equally true is the fact that each brand must discover—and focus on, the particular element which yields the maximum benefit per rupee spent. The driver could be Target group, Product/service, Pricing or Distribution. Brand custodians can then concentrate the marketing efforts—including advertising—around this driver.

To recap the points made in the chapter:

Ask yourself the following questions in order to identify whether you should make the Target Group the driver for your brand:

- *Are there sharply defined, distinct target segments that are being targeted by major brands in our category?*
- *Are there other distinct target segments, which my brand can focus on?*
- *What inputs/support can we employ to focus uniquely on this target segment?*

Ask yourself the following questions in order to identify whether you should make the Product or the Service the driver for your brand:

- *What are the differentiators we will commit to in terms of the product or service?*
- *Do we have patents/intellectual focus/R&D practices and so on to maintain these differentiators?*
- *What are the processes and systems we will adopt to ensure that we retain the power of this driver?*
- *How easily can competitors copy our product or service? How can we make it more difficult for them to copy us?*

Ask yourself the following questions in order to identify whether you should make Pricing the driver for your brand:

- ○ *What do we represent: a different price point or a different Price—Performance Point?*
- ○ *What would happen to our consumers (would we lose them? would they accept it if we increased the price? What if we reduced it?*

Ask yourself the following questions in order to identify whether you should make Distribution the driver for your brand:

- ○ *Are there ways in which consumers access the product/service which are limiting my brand?*
- ○ *Can we do anything to make this access a basis for preference for our brand?*
- ○ *Can we 'protect' these mechanisms from being copied easily?*

By asking these questions related to the different potential drivers for your brand, you will be able to identify the strengths of your brand, and build on them.

A related and very important concept to understand is that the foregoing indicates the importance of understanding the current consumers of your brand. This is a crucial point, because all too often, brand custodians get so focused on attracting new consumers that they forget that the best bet for marketers is to focus on its current users. Better directions for action emerge from understanding why the current consumers choose the brand than from trying to understand why non-users are not choosing it.

To take an example, people who don't like roller-coaster rides may tell you it is because they suffer from vertigo, or that the have a weak heart, and so on; there is not too much you can build on from here. But if the ones who take a ride, and get right back in the queue for another ride tell you that it is the sheer adrenalin rush why they take the ride— well, now you have the driver on which to base the entire marketing programme for the roller coaster rides!

Chapter 3: Action Point Brand Driver Analysis				
	Target Group	*Product or Service*	*Pricing*	*Distribution*
Current				
Brand Driver Assessment				
Potential Driver Approach 1				
Brand Driver Assessment				
Potential Driver Approach 2				
Brand Driver Assessment				

Users and Usage

Identifying the Source of Business

Overview

If you see a man distributing free walnuts at a geriatric convention, there is a good chance that he is in the dentures business!

What is really being said in that remark, is that it is critical to define the characteristics of the prospect group you want to cater to, before you decide your programme of activities, and that the activities must be tailored to the target. Put another way, you aren't going to sell too many combs if you are trying to do it at a bald men's convention!

The above somewhat fanciful example also is intended to indicate that consumer behaviour, consumer practices and consumer habits are what we need to understand, if we are to identify the source of business.

In this chapter we will look at different ways in which we can identify the best source of business for our brand.

There are only two types of potential consumers, in terms of whether they use the product: there are those who are users of the product category and there are those who are not. In terms of the way in which they can possibly use the product, again there are only two choices: to look at the way(s) in which it is currently being used, and possible new ways in which it can be used. (An interesting example is how condensed milk was used as a milk substitute once, until Milkmaid suggested its use as an ingredient to make sweet dishes.)

In this chapter we will look at the four scenarios created by these alternatives, in terms of the challenges they pose and the approaches that can be used to address these situations and build brands.

In an earlier chapter, we looked at competition from the perspective of the product or service characteristics, such as price and technology; which defined alternatives that the prospect could consider. Let us now look at it from the point of the consumer, and how different people take care of their needs.

Let us assume you are managing a brand of shampoo. Now, what might different people be doing to keep their hair clean?

    ○   There will be those who use your shampoo
    ○   Of course there will be those who are using a brand of shampoo other than your brand
    ○   Some people may be using another *product*, such as a soap, which they believe does a decent job of cleaning hair, and see no value in paying more for shampoo
    ○   Others may be choosing to use a service provider, such as a salon, because they think their hair requires special care
    ○   Yet others may be using a homemade product like *shikakai*, which they believe is a healthier way of cleaning hair
    ○   And, a somewhat unusual group (hypothetically speaking) may be choosing to only wash hair with plain water

What we have just done is a simple exercise in which we identified four prospect groups—four sources of business, in the hair-wash market! (We may treat the last group as non-prospects, for this exercise!)

In this chapter, we will look at consumer behaviour, practices and habits to define the source of business for a brand.

The choices available are:

1. Catering to current users of the category and serving current usage patterns.
2. Catering to current users of the category but serving new usage patterns.
3. Catering to new users of the category serving current usage patterns.
4. Catering to new user groups and serving new usage patterns.

Figure 4.1: Strategies for catering to different prospect groups

		Usage Pattern	
		Same	New
Users	Same	1. **Current users, current usage**	2. **Current users, new usage**
	New	3. **New users, current usage**	4. **New users, new usage**

(*Copyright:* Dr. Jagdish N. Sheth, Goizueta Business School, Emory University, Atlanta, GA, USA)

The most effective strategies in each of these situations will be quite different.

Advertising and communication have a very important role in enabling a brand to succeed in these strategies. Let us study them a bit more closely.

1. CURRENT USERS, CURRENT USAGE

This situation is one that you are most likely to encounter. In such a situation, there are a number of brands, all of which cater to similar usage needs. This situation applies in cases such as the toilet soap market, where all brands cater to the same basic need: to clean the skin.

Another such case is that of detergents, which cater to the same basic need to clean clothes. Several other categories, too, face a similar situation.

Product Category	Basic use/need
Hair Oil	Hair grooming and nourishing
Edible Oils	Cooking medium
Shampoos	Hair cleansing
Incandescent Bulbs	Lighting
Refrigerators	Food preservation

Many of the products in these categories—and other categories you may work on—are not vastly different from each other. Yet of course, if they did nothing further about it, there would be a perfect commodity situation and there would be no basis for brand preference; so, obviously, brands do *something* about this me-too world. This is where advertising helps to build competitive differentiation, through a variety of strategies.

Consider which is most appropriate for your brand.

POSITIONING

This has perhaps been the most widely discussed strategy in advertising; ever since the term was introduced by Ries and Trout in the 70s. When several competing products perform—more or less—equally, on the basic category expectation, it is through the process of shaping and managing perceptions, or positioning, that advertising works.

So, Santoor is the soap for youthful skin for years. Dettol is protection against germs. Lux communication is designed to get people to think of it in terms of offering complexion care (it has been placed in the context of film starts, who *need* to look good, to further strengthen the complexion care position).

All of these take the basic need to clean the skin as a given, and consumers do not see this as an area where these brands differ. It is in the areas of complexion care, skin-care and germ-protection and so on, where the differentiation takes place.

Indeed in each of these cases, the basic value of using a soap to cleanse the skin is not even considered in the brand communication; it is the added dimension—such as skin care, which is the focus of communication.

Positioning a brand calls for looking at meaningful, credible extensions of the basic category reasons for usage to create perceived differences. Positioning is a sufficiently important area to merit greater in-depth discussion, and we shall do this in a later chapter.

In the meanwhile, let us look at other strategies, which can be used when your brand is operating in a current user-current usage context.

FOCUS ON HEAVY USERS

In many product categories, a relatively small group of users account for a disproportionately high share of consumption in the category. This phenomenon, often referred to as the '80:20 rule' (about 80 per cent of the usage is accounted for, by about 20 per cent of the users), is valid in categories where there is a wide variation in *per capita* or per family consumption. Some examples of categories in which there is a vide variation in *per-capita consumption*, are: beer, cinema-going, and restaurant-going. Although these are widely different types of categories, you will find that some people in each of these cases are very 'heavy' users, while many others see them only once in a while.

On the other hand in categories like toothpaste, you do not find 'heavy' users and 'light' users, since all users use more or less *similar quantities per -capita*.

In categories where the 80:20 rule operates, heavy users might be the most important source of business and thus acquiring and retaining them would be the appropriate goal for advertising.

Now, consider credit card usage. There is a very wide variation in spends across cardholders. It clearly makes sense for a smaller credit card brand to focus on a heavy spender (rather than attempt to expand the base of users i.e. pursue new users in the category). This is done in several ways. While programmes such as Rewards/Bonus Points are obviously designed to encourage heavy usage, even product variant cues of status and recognition for the heavy user, such as the creation of Gold or Platinum cards, provide a psychological reward.

A similar approach is adopted by Frequent Flyer programmes offered by airlines; where the 'heavy user' is given privileges not available to others:

Figure 4.2: TV commercial: Lux soap

A carnival in progress, two girls are dancing onstage....

Two males admire them from the audience, one of them raves about the girl's skin

The other man (in the jacket) and the viewers presume he is talking about Aishwarya Rai

But it is the other girl (and not Aishwarya Rai) who beckons to them

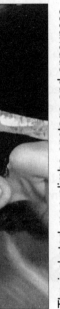

The jacketed man climbs onstage and announces, "Meet my wife!"

VO: "*Naya* Lux Orchid. *Mujhme star jagaye*" (Translation: New Lux Orchid. Awakens the star within me.)

VO: "Orchid *phul aur jojoba* oil *se racha naya* Lux Orchid" (Translation: New Lux Orchid, created with orchid flowers and jojoba oil)

All break into smiles as the girls continue dancing

special departure lounges, special check-in counters, tele-check-in facilities, upgrade vouchers, etc. It is also useful to note that reward systems for the heavy user have a cause and effect impact: they are the *effect* i.e. reward for the heavy usage, but at the same time, they also have a built-in *cause* aspect that works by encouraging the heavy user to continue the heavy usage. It works because once the user gets used to the special privileges, which provide both tangible benefits and status conferred by the reward, the user is loath to let go of them and continues to remain a 'heavy user'—without which he stands to lose the privileges.

Figure 4.3: Press advertisement: Indian Airlines Frequent Flyer Programme

So, while it is often tempting to use advertising to *increase* the number of the user set, in some categories a far better alternative would be to develop a virtuous cycle (Figure 4.4) built by focusing on the heavy user—especially if your brand is not a leader, and you do not have the resources to grow the overall market.

Figure 4.4: Virtuous cycle of focusing on heavy users with loyalty/ reward programme

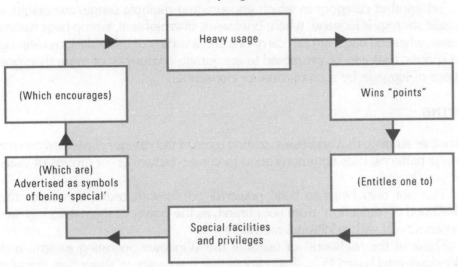

ENCOURAGE MULTIPLE USAGE OR OWNERSHIP

Yet another strategy can be used to address the current usage patterns of current users, when there is a barrier to repeat purchase. This can occur as ownership of a category nears saturation and replacement is low due to the long life and functionality of the product.

Think of wristwatches for example. If you see that almost everyone who could wear a watch is wearing one, what do you do? Just wait until they are ready to replace their watch? Well, maybe you can do something else; you can ask yourself the question: What would it take for the same person to own more than one watch at a time?

An effective strategy, used by Titan watches as penetration of quartz watches increased, was to encourage ownership of more than one watch, through creating different occasion-related appeals. Voila! You have the dress watch, and the sporty watch and the formal watch…and so on. In effect, you have created an 'additional' volume market, by encouraging the building of a 'wardrobe' of watches.

For one, Titan created some very interesting advertising based on this strategy for women's watches. Even recently, the 'What's your style?' campaign featuring Aamir Khan builds on the same idea. For another, Titan also encouraged the gifting of watches to create 'multiple usage'. In fact the exercise was so successful, that as the campaign evolved, the signature tune as someone opened a gift in a TV commercial was enough to tell the viewer that there must be a Titan watch inside the gift-wrapping!

We have also seen in recent times, advertising which encourages a second TV for a youngster, by Videocon.

Yet another category in which encouraging multiple usage/ownership is a valid strategy is luggage, where briefcases, overnighters, laptop bags, vanity cases, wheel-ed bags, aircraft carry-ons and a variety of other designs catering to specific uses can be promoted to encourage ownership of more than one piece of luggage by an individual or household.

TARGETING

Another strategy that addresses existing users of the category based on current usage patterns, uses communication to create 'networks' or groups of users of your brand.

This not only helps to build powerful bonds with users, it reduces the likelihood of 'defection' from your brand, as the power of the network grows exponentially with additional members.

Think of the 'network' of users of the Windows operating system, and Windows-Intel based PCs. If you know that it is easier to share files, transfer data and create LANs using a common operating system and software, it is more likely that the next user will also choose the same basic 'package'.

Hero Motors has created an interesting 'Passport' programme, which creates a sense of belonging and special value for the owners of Hero two-wheelers.

Figure 4.5: Press advertisement: Hero Honda, 'Passport' programme

Maruti Suzuki has created a programme aimed at persuading Maruti owners to select another Maruti as their next car. Ford had a similar programme to encourage trading in an old Ikon for the Nxt model.

It must be noted that while such initiatives can certainly be used as a short-term promotional effort, the value we are discussing comes from seeing them as elements of a long-term strategy. And the initiatives will offer strategic value, when they are 'hooked into' the basic set of associations that the brand owns.

So, for example, the Mahindra Great Escape Rally is a more powerful idea than some of the others discussed. Because it takes (a) the basic idea of a rally with its all-terrain characteristics, (b) links them to the Mahindra brand already known for its ruggedness, power and toughness and then (c) publicly involves the members who belong to the family of Mahindra vehicle owners, in an event which celebrates these very qualities of the brand.

Figure 4.6: Press advertisement: Mahindra, 'Great Escape' promotion

In these approaches and examples we looked at, there were three aspects which were involved.

The first is the *identification of an opportunity*.

In a situation where you are dealing with current users and current usage patterns, the opportunities available may be identified in the following areas:

(a) *Positioning:* In this area think of the perceptions about brands in the category which are negative—can you offer to eliminate them? Think of the benefits being offered by other brands—are there other benefits, which your brand can focus on? The area of Positioning is important enough to be considered separately and will be discussed in detail in a later chapter. But there are other ways you can think of opportunities.

(b) *Heavy vs Light usage:* Are there wide differences in usage patterns? Is there value in focusing on those people who use the product more than the average user, whom we can specifically cater to?

(c) *Multiple usage:* This is another way of looking at usage. Can we look at how to increase usage or ownership in the category?

(d) *Targeting:* Often, there may be opportunities in simply focusing on particular sets of users defined by the brands they use.

Having identified the Opportunity, you will then need to think of what *your strategy* will be. If you have identified the opportunity with rigour, the strategy will follow more or less seamlessly. If not, think about how you can underline the *difference* defined by the opportunity, and how it may be exploited and communicated. For example, if the opportunity is to focus on heavy users, the strategy may be the creation of a Rewards programme, or concentrating on the places that the heavy users visit frequently or building alliances with 'related interest' brands e.g. a music company that produces music CDs may consider a tie-up with a manufacturer of audio equipment.

The third decision you will have to take is to assess *the competitiveness of the opportunity and strategy you have arrived at*. For instance, you may have chosen to address the heavy user i.e. frequent traveller. However, this will be a competitiveness in this approach only if your brand covers routes which account for a very large share of total air traffic—an airline which offers just a few routes, cannot derive much advantage from a Frequent Flyer programme, since its users cannot build up points fast and therefore will not earn much as Rewards!

2. CURRENT USERS, NEW USAGE

Often, the growth in a product category slows to a crawl or almost comes to a stop. This may happen for many reasons.

- o The conditions that created and grew the category may have changed

- There may be a natural *decline in interest* in a product after purchase, which will limit consumption—and therefore, repurchase of the product
- There are products which are purchased for specific reasons, but since *those reasons do not recur* frequently, usage ceases or is low

If the category in which you have a brand is showing slow growth, it may be a category affected by similar developments. If so, you could benefit by considering strategies similar to the ones used by the following brands, which were designed *to build new uses and usage* among current users of the category.

OFFER NEW APPLICATIONS OF THE PRODUCT

Some years ago, Dettol antiseptic liquid faced an unusual problem: although a very high proportion of families had a bottle of Dettol at home, it was used so infrequently that repurchase was low. (Now, here is a category where you can do little to increase consumption: you can hardly suggest to users that they might want to cut or bruise themselves more regularly!)

Equally, advertising to further strengthen Dettol's credentials as an effective antiseptic was not an answer, since the consumers already believed that. So what could the brand do? Well, it found *new applications* for the product: Applications where its antiseptic property had a clear value.

Applications such as adding a little Dettol to the mug of water used while shaving, to provide antiseptic protection on nicks and cuts caused during shaving. Or adding it to the water used to wipe and clean the floors in a house—an idea that was a meaningful extension from the common usage of phenyl as a disinfectant in the washing water. Or adding it in the wash for an infant's cloth nappies, again ensuring that the babies clothes were not only cleaned really well, but were also treated with an antiseptic to kill germs which may be infecting the nappies. These applications were then advertised, and informed people about ways to keep the home and family safe from germs, in situations which went beyond the common, known applications of Dettol for cuts and wounds.

Mobile phone service providers have developed several new uses for existing users in the recent past. Airtel has offered its 'Hello Tunes' facility to permit you to greet callers with your favourite songs. Other services allow the user to download everything from music and ring tones to screen savers, movie clips and film trailers. Yet other services let you get email, news, stock prices, cricket scores, cricket replays, daily horoscopes and a host of other services. In a thought reminiscent of the Tata Steel baseline, 'We also make steel'; one gets the impression that the cellular service providers might well say, 'We also help you make phone calls'!

Another very interesting example of finding new applications for category users comes from one of the elements of the campaign created for the promotion of eggs for the NECC (National Egg Coordination Committee).

Our team at Enterprise Advertising had learnt from consumer research that one of the significant reasons for infrequent consumption of eggs was the perception that there were very few ways of preparing eggs. Most people could not think beyond boiled eggs, omelettes and fried eggs, which got boring after a while.

A very effective part of the campaign was, therefore, communicating through press ads and recipe booklets, the wide variety of ways in which eggs could be eaten: egg korma, egg biryani, egg chaat, and so on. Providing a wide range of reasons to eat eggs, the slogan of this NECC campaign was: 'Sunday ho ya Monday, roz khao andey!' (Translated, the Hindi baseline reads: 'No matter whether it's a Sunday or a Monday, eat eggs everyday'. The author of this book, incidentally, wrote this line.)

Figure 4.7: Press advertisement: NECC, introducing different egg recipes

OFFER PRODUCT LINE EXTENSIONS

Sometimes product extensions require extensive product development work. In other cases, relatively simpler extensions can be leveraged through advertising. One of the key ways in which an extension can drive growth is *expanding opportunities of usage.*

Amongst the simplest ways in which this can be done is introducing new pack sizes/formats. A small pack size, which permits easy 'portability', is obviously able to increase usage opportunities. Examples include the single-lozenge pouches introduced by Vicks Cough Drops and the lower count packs of sanitary protection brands.

However, this is not the only way extensions can expand brand usage. Other methods include the introduction of a new product form. This can be seen in the extension of Dettol antiseptic cream, as an extension of liquid Dettol. Or the introduction of the Iodex spray as an extension of the brand from Iodex, the ointment. By making it easier to carry and use the product, these introductions extend the usage opportunities for the brand.

Yet another way of expanding usage is the introduction of 'take-away' versions i.e. taking the product from its 'home base' to where it is required; this has almost become a basic expectation from restaurants in metro cities, and is the strategic cornerstone of brands such as Domino's pizzas.

Note that the examples mentioned here are *not* examples of brand extensions into new categories—such as Dettol taking the idea of antiseptic protection into soaps. The examples considered here relate to *increasing usage of the same product,* by creating new opportunities for usage (even though Dettol antiseptic cream and Iodex spray do involve product variants, they are still in a very closely related category and address the same basic use).

In this case, the opportunities were identified in the area of new uses, since that is the aspect of consumer behaviour in which you are seeking to bring about change. The opportunities may lie in new ways of using the product or in creating brand extensions that open up new usage opportunities. (In today's marketplace, remember, the marketer is looking for ideas that build business, not only advertising or communication solutions!)

3. NEW USERS, CURRENT USAGE

A third strategy is to target current *non-users* of the category. The options in this strategy include the following:

Geographic Expansion

Obviously, one way of reaching current non-users is to go beyond the current ambit of marketing efforts, for example to go beyond the existing urban users of a brand, and reach rural users in the target group. This is more than simply a matter of extending distribution, as it may appear on the surface. This is because the extension may have important implications for advertising, as the brand starts addressing new users, even if the change is primarily built around geographic expansion.

A striking recent example of this is the strategy adopted by Coca Cola in 2003. Company spokesmen have explained that they saw the *'Paanch matlab chota* Coke' (Five means the small Coke) and *'Thanda matlab* Coca Cola' advertising as being directed toward rural/semi-urban consumers, while the *'Piyo Thanda, Jiyo Thanda'* advertising has been developed to appeal to urban prospects. (There has been some reconsideration of the strategy in 2004, and some question marks on the profitability of the initiative, but the fact remains that it was a strategy aimed at targeting new users.) The TV commercial (Figure 4.8) for the same, focuses on the price of Coca Cola i.e. Rs 5.

Other recent examples have been the expansion of regional brands like Medimix from Kerala, into the 'national' arena. The change in advertising accompanying this strategy is striking, as the brand extends its appeal. The advertising appeal has taken on a pan-Indian expression, from a strongly regional one, although the raison d'etre of the brand as representing ayurvedic skin-care ingredients remains unchanged.

Generic Marketing to New Segments

A second, very useful approach is to *address a new segment* of users through advertising, without necessarily creating fundamentally new products.

Titan Industries created the 'Dash' range of wristwatches to specifically target kids. Until a few years ago, watches had targeted adults, with school leaving/college-admission time as the 'entry-point' for watches. Actually what Titan did was to *reflect* and magnify a change that was already taking place in the world around it; i.e. the lower age at which parents were buying watches for their children.

Other recent examples can be seen in the financial services area, as insurance companies and credit card brands target women as prospects.

Yet another, very interesting example is to be seen in mobile phones. As the category moves from being a status symbol of the elite, to business tool, to a lifestyle accessory, the focus has clearly shifted to advertising that is aimed at the youth. And the advertising for both mobile phone handsets and cellular service providers reflects this new focus.

INSTITUTIONAL-TO-DOMESTIC OR DOMESTIC-TO-INSTITUTIONAL USER SHIFT

This is another way to attract new users with the same basic product.

Perhaps the most significant shift in focus from institutional to domestic users has been seen in PCs. As computer literacy becomes an essential skill, this has created a large, key new source of business for computer hardware and software brands. From the earlier selling of PCs largely to office and business users, the efforts have changed to targeting young home users (see Figure 4.9).

When you are seeking new users for using the product in more or less the same way as current users of the brand or category, the focus of your efforts would be looking for geographic expansion opportunities, for gaining a first-mover advantage by creating generic acceptance or demand for the product or service, or by a shift in focus from an institutional market to an individual market (or vice versa).

Of course as before, you have to be sure that the 'offer' you have put together is not only competitive but also 'ownable', in that its benefits can continue to be harvested by your brand, and not go to others. For example, if a small toothpaste brand attempted an exercise to convert users of toothpowder to toothpastes, chances are that the advantage would go to a dominant brand like Colgate, and not to the small brand that initiated the exercise.

4. NEW USERS, NEW USES

This is the 'boldest' strategy in terms of choosing the source of business for your brand. Yet it is not as difficult as may appear at first glance. Here are some ways in which it can be done.

REPOSITIONING

Complan has been one of the most interesting cases of repositioning. Complan, formulated with 23 vital nutrients, is excellent for convalescents, persons in need of nutritional supplementation and for those unable to eat/ digest a normal diet. And it was for these specific-situation uses that the brand was promoted in the 1970s and early 1980s. The limitation in this

Figure 4.8: TV commercial: Coca Cola 'Five means (the) small Coke'

Two village belles ask for a thanda at a road-side *dhaba* even as a traveller is shown washing his hands at a tubewell...

...pump. On hearing the *dhaba* owner charging six rupees for the *chota* Coke, he promptly comes to the rescue of the girls.

He confronts the shopkeeper, who in turn, gets very miffed. To drive home the point of Coke being only for rupees five, the *babu*...

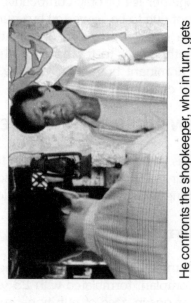

...lets loose a flurry of questions, (fingers *kitne hain, pandav kitne the*, etc.). Caught in this barrage of five...

Correcting himself, the shopkeeper lifts one finger. The *babu* nods and asks him to return 1 rupee.

...and sings out," *Arre thande ka tadka lagai diya re, harmonia bajaike".* In the backdrop of the song, MVO: *"Paanch matlab chhota Coke."*

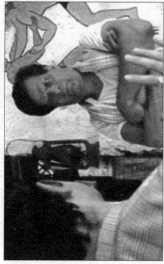

...related questions, he blurts out five even when asked for the number of fathers he has.

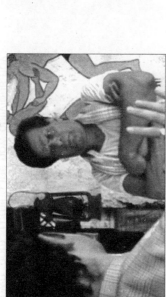

Then as he gets ready to resume his journey, the good samaritan puts on his sunglasses, gives a knowing nod to the girls...

Figure 4.9: TV commercial: Compaq computers

A girl is about to sneak back into her home, way past her curfew, when she spots her dad waiting for her to show up.

An idea strikes her and she extracts a wireless mouse from her purse with an impish grin. She returns to her waiting date...

...to operate the computer perched inside her room and creates the sound of vessels crashsing. Her dad assumes...

...and guides him outside the window of her own room. Turning the now oblivious boy towards her, she uses the mouse...

...to wait outside as she sneaks in.
MVO: "A wireless mouse feature with the
new Compaq Presario 7000 and Pentium
IV processor."

...after 'creating' the sound of the door bell,
with her Compaq. MVO: "Delivers
performance, when you need it the most."

...that it comes from the kitchen and hurries
to check. The coast is now clear for the girl
to tiptoe inside. She requests her date...

The doorbell chimes and her dad opens it to
see the boy waiting to be summoned inside.
Cut to her room, the girl bursts into laughter...

Figure 4.10: TV commercial: Complan (2004)

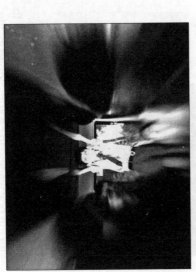

Inside a school bus, Boy1 is swinging on the handlebar overhead.

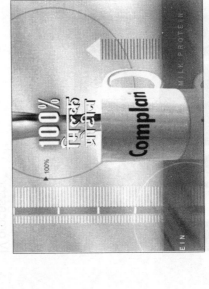

Boy 2 says: "You are not going to grow taller just by swinging like this!"

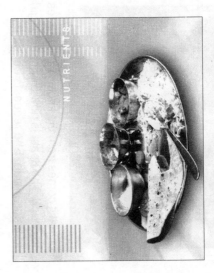

VO: If your child doesn't eat properly, how will he get essential nutrition and proteins?

VO: Complan has 100 per cent milk protein and 23 essential nutrients, which give extra growing power.

VO: Complan. Extra growing power, in tasty flavours.

"Yes" says Boy1 proudly, and demonstrates how he has become taller....

Next day the two meet again: "Not swinging anymore? Is your Mom giving you Complan now?"

Excitedly, he continues, "Now I am a Complan boy!"

strategy was the fact that the brand did not have a large base of regular users. In a comprehensive exercise, Complan was repositioned as a 'complete food for growing children': It took the same product and presented its benefit in a manner relevant to a different set of users (see Figure 4.10) to create a much larger, regular source of business.

Another brand, which executed an effective repositioning strategy, was Milkmaid. Milkmaid condensed milk was often a 'milk-substitute in an emergency' during the days of milk shortage. Consumers would reconstitute it to create liquid milk, when fresh milk was not available. However, as milk availability improved across India, following the success of Operation Flood, Milkmaid's very raison d'être was in danger of redundancy!

The innovative solution, which was backed by simple, focused advertising, was to reposition it as an *ingredient for easy to prepare sweet dishes.* Advertising, pack labels, recipe booklets, all worked in this direction, and Milkmaid became the 'ingredient X' of *gulab jamun, gajar halwa* and *kheer.*

Although repositioning can be used to attract new users through new uses, this strategy is likely to be far more effective when the effort rests on the back of a genuine product innovation and alters the category dynamics. Innovations of this type include the introduction of the pocket calculator from the desk calculator and tea bags as an innovation, different from leaf tea.

As noted above, to seek new consumers *and* to offer them new ways of using the product is tantamount to creating a new category! Repositioning is one way to do this, short of introducing significant product modifications.

SOURCE OF BUSINESS ANALYSIS

Before proceeding to the next chapter, assess your brand's users and usage and fill out the Source of Business Matrix. Consider options in all the four cells before deciding which one offers the greatest potential to grow your business.

Given here, as thought-starters, are examples for each of the four situations discussed.

Example 1: Source of business analysis. Current users, current usage

---

Current users, current usage: Revlon lipstick

- *Opportunity:* To differentiate brand by adding do-good value to 'decorative' properties of the product
- *Strategy:* Position the lipsticks as 'the lipstick with lip protection', based on the moisturizer property of the product
- *Competitive edge:* Credibility of brand in cosmetics and perceived product category expertise allows brand to claim new high ground

---

Example 2: Source of business analysis. Current users, new usage

---

Current users, new usage: Nescafe

- *Opportunity:* To promote consumption in summer months when consumption of hot beverages (tea and coffee) tends to drop

- *Strategy:* Create special promotion and communication during summer to promote consumption of *cold* coffee

- *Competitive edge:* Nescafe as the leader in the instant coffee category, is the one most likely to benefit from the generic use promotion

---

Example 3: Source of business analysis. New users, current usage

---

New users, current usage: ICICI Credit Cards

- *Opportunity:* To become the first credit card of new users, who can then become life-time customers for the brand

- *Strategy:* Introduce a 'Students Card' (which is backed by a parent with the earning capacity), to gain entry-level usage among youngsters

- *Competitive edge:* The high awareness, 'aggressive, contemporary' image, and strong ATM network of the bank likely to make it the preferred choice of the urban young

---

Example 4: Source of business analysis. New users, new usage

New users, new usage: Asmi diamonds

- *Opportunity:* To extend usage of diamonds to regular day-wear jewellery, (instead of remaining restricted to the traditional wedding ring and jewellery)

- *Strategy:* Promote affordable diamond jewellery as the choice of the independent young woman, who is not bound by traditional notions

- *Competitive edge:* Can establish a perceived point of difference in a category in which it is difficult to establish brand differences

---

In this chapter, we looked at competition from the perspective of the consumer and how different people take care of their needs.

We looked at how the use patterns for the product or service, may range all the way from:

- There will be those who use your brand
- *Those who are using another brand*
- *Those who are using another product, which they believe does more or less the same job*
- *Those who are using a specialist service provider to fulfil the need, to:*
- *Those who are using a homemade product*

When we look at this spectrum of usage patterns, along with the fact that there are also different ways in which people use products, it becomes clear that the choices available to a marketer to grow business are:

- *Catering to current users of the category and serving current usage patterns.*
- *Catering to current users of the category but serving new usage patterns.*
- *Catering to new users of the category serving current usage patterns.*
- *Catering to new user groups and serving new usage patterns.*

We saw that as you plan the advertising for your brand, therefore, it is necessary to consider each of these situations with reference to your brand, and to ask yourself:

- *What is the opportunity available?*
- *What is likely to be the competition the brand will face?*
- *And what is the competitive advantage that the brand can build or leverage to capitalize on the identified opportunity?*

We saw that the nature of the opportunity will vary in each of the four situations described.

Having identified the opportunity, we saw that we next need to think of what the strategy will be, and that if the opportunity has been identified with rigour, the strategy will follow more or less seamlessly.

Finally, we saw that the third area to consider is to assess the competitiveness of the opportunity and strategy arrived at.

Chapter 4: Action Point
Source of Business Analysis

1. **Current users, current usage**	2. **Current users, new usage**
• Opportunity:	• Opportunity:
• Strategy:	• Strategy:
• Competitive edge:	• Competitive edge:
3. **New users, current usage**	4. **New users, new usage**
• Opportunity:	• Opportunity:
• Strategy:	• Strategy:
• Competitive edge:	• Competitive edge:

Segmentation

Defining the Dimensions of Target Groups

Overview

Hippies were members of the 1960s counterculture movement who adopted a communal or nomadic lifestyle, renounced corporate nationalism and the Vietnam War, embraced aspects of Buddhism, Hinduism, and/or Native American religious culture, and were otherwise at odds with traditional middle class Western values. They saw paternalistic government, corporate industry, and traditional social mores as part of a unified establishment that had no authentic legitimacy.

Other traits associated with hippies included clothes having bright colors, and certain unusual styles (such as bell-bottom pants, tie-dyed shirts, peasant blouses, and Indian-inspired clothing), listening to certain styles of music; psychedelic rock such as the Grateful Dead, Jefferson Airplane, Janis Joplin, performing music casually, in friends' homes, or for free at outdoor fairs such as San Francisco's legendary 'Human Be-In' of January 1967 and Woodstock (a famous gathering attended mostly by hippies), free love, communal living and the use of recreational drugs, particularly marijuana, hashish, and hallucinogens such as LSD and Psilocybin. Marijuana was prized as much for its iconoclastic, illicit nature as for its psycho-pharmaceutical effects.

~ from Wikipedia, *the free encyclopedia.*

In this chapter we will be looking at segmentation: the decision about the group at whom we will target for our marketing efforts. The reason why it is necessary to choose a target group, rather than the entire universe is quite simply based on the fact that if you try to appeal to everyone's tastes and preferences, you are likely to end up appealing to no one. Consider a simple example. Imagine that you are a maker of garments. Now what kind of clothes would you produce if you wanted to appeal to the hippies described above? And would the same clothes then be appealing to a conservative banker on Wall Street? Not likely, right? Exactly. That is why you need to decide which segment you want to target: the hippie segment or the banker segment.

In this chapter we will look at the various parameters we can consider, in order to define target groups and the aspects to consider in deciding which basis is the appropriate one for your brand.

The fundamental purpose of segmentation is to concentrate your marketing and advertising efforts. The opposite of 'segmentation', which you will not find in a list of antonyms, is 'unfocused'. In the early days of demand exceeding supply, and relatively few brands, a brand could attempt to be all things to all people, but in today's markets with a host of competitors, a brand which tries to be everything to everyone, is more likely to end up meaning nothing to anyone.

Segmentation is *the process of defining internally homogenous and externally heterogeneous groups that can be reached by customized marketing plans*. The lifestyle of hippies described above clearly defines them as a homogenous group with its own defined characteristics.

Think, for a moment, of the archetypal Hindi film potboiler that is luridly advertised as offering 'A romantic, action-packed family musical story of betrayal and revenge.' It says everything—and thus—nothing! Sounds like something you would not expect to see being done by marketing communication professionals, right?

Yet, consider this fairly typical example from an advertising brief, and you will see a similar lack of focus

'Target group for XYZ shampoos (it could as easily be DEF talc or RST moisturiser): 18-45 year old women from SEC A, B and C in urban areas.'

Romance, action, family… all of it seems to be here too. Before going further, pause and write down the target group definition of your brand.

Target group:

_____

_____

_____

Done? Good. It will help you appreciate what follows.

SEGMENTATION BY DEMOGRAPHIC GROUPS

There are two key aspects of demographic segmentation that you should be careful about:

1. MEMBERS OF A TARGET GROUP MUST BE SIMILAR

The first factor to look at is 'internal homogeneity' i.e. are the people *within* the group you have chosen to target, sufficiently *similar*? This seems obvious, but be critical in examining your assumptions. What you must look at is whether you can expect the members of the group you have defined to be similar, or are there are logical valid reasons *to expect differences* within your defined group.

This is critical, because such differences defeat the very objective of segmentation. Groups defined by a demographic, say age, often hide the differences between the members of the group. This happens because while the group may be similar in terms of the selected demographic definition, their behaviour and thinking may be guided by some other factor, on which the members of your group are *dissimilar.*

Let us look again at our illustrative example: 18-45 year old women from SEC A, B and C in urban areas. How *internally homogenous* is the target group as defined? When one considers the age band of 18-45 years, say for a brand of shampoo, one might consider that there are likely to be wide differences in women's behaviour and thinking across this band, which is not reflected in age, but by their stage in life. Important life-situation differences are hidden when traditional breaks such as 18-25, 26-35 and so on are used. Such a wide range of life-situations, will almost certainly be reflected in different considerations about the needs, expectations, priorities, etc. related to the shampoo they choose. This might suggest that you should recast the data with these values, to confirm that age in fact is the defining variable.

Table 5.1: Different needs at different life stages

Age	Likely occupation	Likely marital status	Likely family scenario	Likely needs/ concerns
18-20	Student (undergraduate)	Unmarried	Living with parents or in hostel	Shine, bounce, no dandruff
21-22	Post-graduate student, working, or unemployed	Unmarried	Living with parents or in a hostel	Shine, softness, manageability
23-25	Working housewife	Married	No children	Manageability, nourishment
26-32	Working housewife	Married	Children in pre-school stage	Manageability, fight premature graying
33-42	Working housewife	Married	School going children	Nourishment, suitability for entire family
43-45	Working housewife	Married	College-going children	Graying, hair fall

In fact, demographics as the basis of segmentation are often ineffective for precisely the type of variations, which we saw in the preceding example of the high degree of heterogeneity *within* demographic segments.

The Co-existence of Multiple Product Life Cycles (PLCs): One can get a better understanding of the limitations of demographics to define segments by thinking in terms of the co-existence of multiple Product Life Cycles.

The concept of Product Life Cycle is *most applicable at the product or category level,* and classically, the product category is assumed to go through a change in the penetration or usage level over time. The classic Product Life Cycle curve is as shown in the figure below.

PENETRATION

Figure 5.1: The classic Product Life Cycle

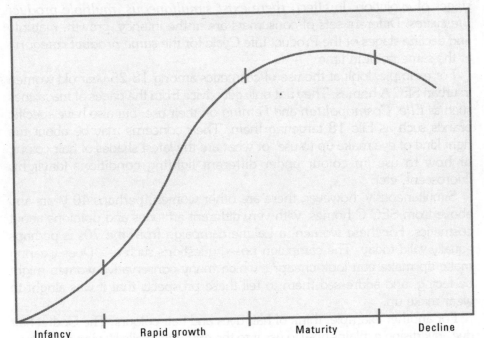

| Infancy | Rapid growth | Maturity | Decline |

While the phenomenon of Product Life Cycle operates at the product category level, it has definite implications for *brands*, because the consumer orientation, and the relative focus of communication is different at the various stages of the Product Life Cycle (Table 5.2).

Table 5.2: Product Life Cycle and changing communication focus

	Competitive context	*Focus of communication*
Infancy	Category competition	Superiority over *category* being replaced
Rapid growth	Some competitors	Establishing different bases for brand preference
Maturity	Many competitors	Superiority over competition
Decline	Many competitors, little product difference	Promotions, price offs, etc

(*Copyright*: Dr. Jagdish N. Sheth, Goizueta Business School, Emory University, Atlanta, GA, USA)

If only life were so simple!

One of the important consequences of the state of evolution and flux in the Indian market is that there are large numbers of consumers at the different stages of evolution. In effect, *there exist simultaneous, multiple product life cycles*. Different sets of consumers are at the infancy, growth, maturity and decline stages of the Product Life Cycle for the *same product category*, at the same point in time.

For example, look at the use of cosmetics among 18-25 year old women in urban SEC A homes. They not only get advice from the pages of magazines such as *Elle, Cosmopolitan* and *Femina* on their use, but also have specific brands such as Elle 18 targeting them. Their concerns may be about the right kind of eye make up to use, or what are the latest shades of hair colour, or how to use lip colour under different lighting conditions (daylight, fluoroscent, etc).

Simultaneously, however, there are other women, perhaps 40 years and above from SEC C homes, with very different attitudes and opinions about cosmetics. For these women, a Lakme campaign from the 70s is perhaps equally valid today. The campaign posed questions such as: 'Does wearing make up make you look cheap?', which many conservative women might be facing, and addressed them to tell these prospects that it was alright to wear make up.

For another example, think of hair dyes and hair colours. The Godrej hair dye advertising explains how to use it to the entrants, while Revlon or L'Oreal hair colour communication takes all this for granted. The issue is that the advertiser needs to be clear whom she wishes to address, rather than attempt a one-size-will-fit-all approach.

This phenomenon is important, and a brand must be aware of these 'simultaneous Product Life Cycles', before deciding which segment to focus on. You can get a very good idea of the existence of such simultaneous

Figure 5.2: Press advertisement: Elle 18, reflecting the attitudes of teenagers

Product Life Cycles, by considering the penetration of some product categories among consumer segments defined by different variables such as age, SEC and education.

Think of the women described by age, SEC and education in Table 5.3 (The groups have deliberately been defined in non-contiguous ways). Now, what percentage of the women in each of the columns would you guesstimate to be users of products listed? Don't worry about whether you have access to the actual data—just apply your judgment. Write down whether you think the percentage is High, Medium or Low. Do you think the usage of Deodorant sprays in the age group 16-22 is high? What about women aged 40+? Go ahead; take a few minutes to arrive at your estimate…

Your assessment will give you a sense of the existence of simultaneous Product Life Cycles for different segments, and why this ought to be one of the basic variables to consider in the segmentation decision for a brand.

It is this heterogeneity, within conventionally defined demographic segments that can make demographic-based segmentation ineffective

Demographics, unfortunately, is the most common basis available for *media planning* (though even there, product usage and other data can be used to refine targeting). And because demographic definitions of target group are arrived at for media planning decisions, they have an insidious way of finding their way into *advertising planning*.

Table 5.3: Estimating product usage

Usage	Age			Sec			Education		
	16-22 Unmarried	26-35	40+	A	C	D	Below SSC	Some college not graduate	Post Grad.
Deodorants									
Sprays									
Talc									
Hair Colour									
Use									
Cosmetics									
Use only lipstick									
Use lipstick + blushers and/ or eye make up									
Whitener in Tea/Coffee									
Use dairy whitener									
Use milk in tetrapak cartons									
Use regular wet milk									

You must be very careful to watch out against this. Perhaps an analogy might help. You might use 'demographic' classifications such as 'office colleagues', 'class mates', 'fellow club members', etc. to order your address book. But that is not necessarily the basis you use to decide the guest list for a party! For that, you might look at some other aspects about people, which cut *across these 'sets'* such as whether they enjoy dancing!

This is not to say that there is no place for demographic segmentation. There are several product categories where it is certainly valid:

- ○ Infants, as a segment for skin care, soap and talc
- ○ School children and their parents, as a segment for school bags, shoes etc.
- ○ Students at specific stages of education, for computer and other vocational training courses

There will be other situations where income may very well be the most important basis of segmentation. For instance, in marketing different investment options. However, in most product categories you are likely to work on, demographic variables may not be the best discriminants of behaviour.

The key point to note is that demographics (or any other variable, for that matter) are a valid basis for segmentation, *only if the demographic characteristic is an important determinant of thinking and behaviour in relation to the product category and your brand*. If not, you may be using it more out of habit and past definitions, and may need to reexamine your segmentation analysis.

2. DEFINITIONS MUST DISCRIMINATE

The second aspect to look at is the 'discriminating power' of your definitions. The whole point of segmentation, of arriving at 'externally heterogeneous' groups is defeated, if the definitions and variables do not *discriminate across groups*.

Consider the earlier example. Why cut-off the age at 45 years? Is there reason to believe that there is a significant drop in usage of shampoo after that age? If it is not so, why not consider the age group of 18–50 years as your target group? Or, for that matter, why not the age group of 18–60 years? In fact one might legitimately ask: is there any need to use age as a defining criterion at all?

Examine the value of the SEC definition. Look at whether there is a difference between women in say, SEC A and B on the one hand and SEC C on the other. Is there a case for actually dropping SEC C from the target group definition?

Carry out a simple exercise to check if the group you have defined is actually *discriminating*. Here is how to do it, using the above illustration. (Note: The data itself is hypothetical.)

Let us begin by looking at just two measures: the percentage of population represented by each of these groups and the penetration of the category in each.

Table 5.4: Assessment of penetration of category by age groups

	All urban women (above 15 years)	All 18-45 year old urban women	Urban women under 18 or above 45 years
Percentage Population (Horizontal total = 100)	100	65	35
Penetration of category (i.e. percentage of the population group defined in each column who use the category)	25	32	12

The above table seems to suggest that there is nothing wrong with the definition we looked at earlier i.e. targeting the 18-45 year old; after all, the usage of the category *among these women is 32 per cent*—much higher than for the women *outside* this age band, only 12 per cent of whom use the category.

Yet, let us look at this age group of 18-45 years a little more closely. Now, *split* the 18-45 year olds into three age groups: 18-25, 26-35 and 35-45, and look at the penetration data.

Table 5.5: Assessment of penetration of category by split age groups

	All urban women (above 15)	All 18-45 year old urban women	18-25 year old urban women	26-35 year old urban women	36-45 year old urban women	Urban women under 18 or above 45
Percentage of Population (Horizontal total = 100)	100	65	25	20	20	35
Penetration of category (i.e. percentage of the population group defined in each column who use the category)	25	32	40	35	20	12

Suddenly it doesn't look so simple, does it? In fact what the data is showing is that you should perhaps be limiting the target group definition to *18-35 year* old women, since the penetration drops quite sharply to only 20 per cent in the 36-45 year group. So should you adopt 18-35 year olds as your target group?

Let us look at one more input: the share of your brand in these groups.

Table 5.6: Share of brand among age groups

	All urban women (above 15 years)	All 18-45 year old urban women	18-25 year old urban women	26-35 year old urban women	36-45 year old urban women	Urban women under 18 or above 45
Percentage of Population (Horizontal total = 100)	100	65	25	20	20	35
Penetration of category (i.e. percentage of the population group defined in each column who use the category)	25	32	40	35	20	12
Percentage share of your brand among users in each column	27	28	10	**40**	**50**	25

This input (Table 5.6) tells us something very interesting. It tells us that while on a *category penetration basis* the 18-35 year old group is the most important, on a brand share basis, the *26-45 year olds group is where your business is strongest*: So if your main objective is to protect your current franchise, it is this group you must target!

This simple example illustrates how important it is to 'slice and dice' the population in different ways before you form a judgment about the specific group you want to target. More importantly, it will allow you to *consider the importance of different dimensions* of segmenting the population before you decide which dimension is the critical one for you.

Carry out similar exercises for other dimensions, such as the SEC groups, which you have used to define your target. If the cut-offs you have used do not actually reveal differences, the description is not *discriminating* between the defined group and the rest of the population and is not a meaningful way to define your target group.

Table 5.7: Exercise on penetration of category by SEC

	All urban women (above 15 years)	SEC A & B	SEC C	SEC D & E
Percentage of Population				
Penetration of category (i.e. percentage of the population group defined in each column who use the category)				
Percentage share of your brand among users in each column				

Yet, demographics are not the only basis on which you can define target groups. (It is assumed that you have already done the source of business analysis, and have decided which group, in terms of usage, you will be targeting.) Here are some other ways in which you can define segments.

SEGMENTATION BY NEED/BENEFIT CONSIDERATION

If there is a specific need that a section of the population considers more important, it can be the basis of segmentation for your brand. Very often, the need being served or benefit being offered will be something *latent* rather than overt, since the *overt, basic need* usually is being catered to, by the category leader brand. Very often, it is also the strategy a new entrant *has* to adopt to compete in an established category.

Take shampoos. Clinic All Clear established leadership by offering a solution against dandruff, a specific benefit that goes beyond cleansing hair. Another new benefit, which helped other new entrants, was the promise of 'nourishment' of hair by shampoos, by promising a benefit earlier associated with only hair oils. Shampoo users have thus been segmented into 'I need to fight dandruff' and 'I need to nourish my hair' need segments.

A similar pattern can be seen in dental care. Colgate Dental Cream, the leader in toothpastes in India, for many years, represented the 'umbrella' benefits of toothpaste: fights bad breath, helps prevent tooth decay.

Competing brands over the years, took up more specific benefits to address specific need segments.

Table 5.8: Need benefits in toothpastes

Need	Brands
Gum care	Forhans, Pepsodent G
Children's dental care	Signal, Pepsodent
Sparkling white teeth, fresh breath	Close up
Strong teeth	Vicco Vajradanti

A very dramatic illustration of segmentation by need/benefit is employed in the promotion of travel destinations. Very clearly, the things people look for in a holiday vary widely, creating different segments, some of which are shown in the table below.

Table 5.9: Need benefits in travel destinations

Benefit sought	'Brands' offering benefit
'Get away from it all tranquility'	Club Med, Maldives
Natural beauty	Kerala, wildlife sanctuaries, Himachal Pradesh
Excitement, fun	Disneyland, Las Vegas
Exotic experiences	Angkor Wat, Sikkim, Andaman Islands
Romance of history	Rajasthan
Religious experience	Hardwar, Amarnath, Tirupati, Nashik (Trimbakeshwar)

Even the same advertiser will find it necessary to offer different holiday experiences to cater to different benefits sought by tourists. Consider the Maharashtra Tourism campaign that offered different experiences to people who seek different pleasures.

However, it is necessary to note that segmentation by needs or benefits is becoming less and less likely to build powerful brands today. This is because there are only a limited number of genuinely different significant needs in any category.

Let us go back to the example of toothpastes we looked at earlier. Gum care, care for children's teeth, fresh breath, strong teeth. Now, how many other needs can you think of? Perhaps you say, 'prevention of tooth decay'. Next?

Figure 5.4: Press advertisement: Maharashtra Tourism, based on appeal of the mountains

Figure 5.3: Press advertisement: Maharashtra Tourism, based on appeal of the sea

Maybe you say, 'a special toothpaste for people with sensitive teeth'. OK. Next?

The point being made is, there are only a few dramatically different needs in dental care. Yes of course, you can start developing more refined differences. For example, one might think of 'whitening yellow teeth'. How different is that from 'sparkling white teeth'? Fairly soon you will fall prey to the temptation to define differences which are more in the semantics than in the fact. And how different a need will the eleventh toothpaste serve?

The same is true for most categories that have been around for any length of time.

Let us think of detergents. The important needs which consumers have are:

- ○ Getting clothes sparkling white
- ○ Getting coloured clothes clean and bright
- ○ Removing stains

You might say there is also 'cleaning without letting white turn yellow'. This is really a variation of the first need noted above, isn't it? You might say there is another benefit such as, 'getting stains out without the colour fading'. This is a variant of the second need/benefit noted above.

To seek further differences, one can think of:

- ○ Adding a fresh fragrance
- ○ Being gentle on the hands
- ○ Not damaging clothes
- ○ Cleaning well, at a low or reasonable cost

Now one is either beginning to create what at best are 'additional' benefits such as added fragrance or defining benefits by negation i.e. based on the *elimination of negatives*, such as not damaging clothes. You can see how these 'benefits' are intrinsically weaker than the central benefits. And if there are attempts to define even more benefits, you will be compelled to arrive at even more 'distant' needs/benefits.

Let us consider one last example in this area: health beverages.

The important benefits revolve around growth (physical and mental), energy (physical and mental) and variations thereof. Brands may attempt to create differences through presenting a case that one particular brand meets all the Required Daily Allowances, another may focus on the extra calcium it has and another may speak of being protein-rich. But these are ways of creating *positioning differences, not catering to different needs*.

We will look at positioning differences in Chapter 8 in detail. Suffice it here to note that as competition grows and there are more brands in a particular category, defining segments by significantly different needs (or benefits) becomes more and more difficult, and in fact less meaningful from a consumer perspective.

SEGMENTATION BY USAGE HABITS/PRACTICES

A variation of segmentation by need/benefit, is the notion of segmentation by usage habit/practice. Fundamentally, this is also a way of serving a different need, but is worth looking at a separate basis for segmentation since the *need itself arises from specific usage* habits.

In many categories, a host of different usage patterns can be observed, and these can offer opportunities for segmentation. Here are some examples.

Using soap for hair & body wash: A fairly large part of the population used toilet soaps to also wash hair, until not so long ago. Although this has probably become less common now, it represented a clear segment. This was the segment addressed by a brand such as Godrej's Crowning Glory.

Paan chewing & smoking: These obviously have an effect on the appearance of teeth and the freshness of breath, and offer opportunities for segmentation, for say, a special toothpaste designed to remove stains caused by these habits.

But again, there are only a few usage patterns in any area, and thus new brands in highly competitive categories will need to find other ways to define target segments.

Perhaps the most useful way to do this is to look at what is happening in the mind and heart of consumers, and segment them by their attitudes and beliefs.

SEGMENTATION BY BELIEFS/ATTITUDES OF PROSPECT

As we saw above, when you run out of different needs to cater to, think of what differentiates people in terms of *their thinking*.

To get a vivid sense of the fact that consumers respond to appeals that involve their beliefs, attitudes and thinking, let us look at the brands rated in surveys by *brandchannel.com*, the website created and managed by Interbrand. The annual Readers' Choice Awards conducted by the website recognize the brands that have the most impact each year.

Here are the top 20 Global winners of the 2004 Readers' Choice Awards survey:

1. Apple
2. Google

3. Ikea
4. Starbucks
5. Al Jazeera
6. Mini
7. Coca-Cola
8. Virgin
9. eBay
10. Nokia
11. Sony
12. H&M (Hennes & Mauritz)
13. BMW
14. Puma
15. Zara
16. Samsung
17. Nike
18. Amazon.com
19. Olympics
20. Yahoo!

You can see that the list does not include most of the brands, which make it to the top of the World's Most Valuable Brands list. Yet, since they represent the Readers' Choice, they must be close to their hearts. Here are some of the explanations for the appeal of these brands, as assessed by observers and Brandchannel.com itself.

Apple has what John Schwartz in the *New York Times* described as the '*attitude of an artist and the eye of an anthropologist*' (16 January 2005) even though it has less than a two per cent share of the world market as a computer brand.

About Sir Richard Branson's Virgin brand, the website says, 'Richard Branson continues to delight or disgust depending on one's perspective, but we suspect the voters for Virgin in this ranking are definitely fans. Sir Richard's tremendous talent *for making us feel like winners just for choosing Virgin* cannot be underestimated.'

(The author has italicized some words in the quotes, for emphasis.)

In Asia-Pacific, many consumers are still discovering the joy of great technology and service, as you can see when you look at the top brands in the same Readers' Choice Awards for this region:

1. Sony
2. Samsung
3. LG Electronics
4. Toyota

5. Lonely Planet
6. Singapore Airlines
7. HSBC
8. Honda
9. Qantas
10. nudie drinks

But cult personality brands are big in the US and Canada regions (where we know marketing and advertising is far more competitive and has had to go beyond product and technology features). The flamboyant, adventurous real estate and reality TV developer Donald Trump is ranked seventh, with lifestyle and home personality Martha Stewart next at rank eight and talk show host and TV icon Oprah Winfrey at ten.

You can see that brands that capture, express and in fact *represent* emotionally rich points of view and attitude can rise beyond their market share, and appeal to groups of people who share that view or attitude.

There are many brands that have used such a segmentation strategy based on beliefs/attitudes of groups. Here are some examples.

NATURAL/HERBAL-HEALTH-CARE CONSCIOUSNESS

Several brands target the segment of people with a strong faith in natural, chemical-free, solutions. These include Biotique, Vatika and Vicco in India, and, internationally, The Body Shop. Consider the following extract from The Body Shop website:

PROFITS WITH PRINCIPLES: THE BODY SHOP MISSION STATEMENT

The Body Shop is on a never-ending journey. We will never be satisfied with the status quo. We will never be perfect. The work that we're doing is never done. It always gets more challenging. It always gets better. That's the exciting part.

The only thing that will stay the same at The Body Shop is what we believe in—Profits With Principles. We strive to change everything else to maintain creative positive change. We at The Body Shop will continue to challenge ourselves, our industry, our staff, and our customers.

Because business should be anything but the usual.

We hope you will join us in this adventure.

MISSION STATEMENT—OUR REASON FOR BEING

To dedicate our business to the pursuit of social and environmental change.

To Creatively balance the financial and human needs of our stakeholders: employees, franchisees, customers, suppliers and shareholders.

To Courageously ensure that our business is ecologically sustainable: meeting the needs of the present without compromising the future.

To Meaningfully contribute to local, national and international communities in which we trade, by adopting a code of conduct which ensures care, honesty, fairness and respect.

To Passionately campaign for the protection of the environment, human and civil rights, and against animal testing within the cosmetics and toiletries industry.

To Tirelessly work to narrow the gap between principle and practice, whilst making fun, passion and care part of our daily lives.

THE MEN (AND WOMEN) OF PRINCIPLE AND INTEGRITY

This is an attitude that has always been desired by a segment of people.

A TV commercial for Bajaj Caliber motorcycles a few years ago showed a young man who stops at a traffic light when it turns red. A politician or Government official's cavalcade of cars is approaching, and a rough 'party worker' wants the young man to move his motorcycle, because it is going to obstruct the movement of the cars. The young man just looks at the traffic light and refuses to back down. The cavalcade is brought to a stop, but the young man moves off only after the traffic signal turns green. He is the man who will do the right thing no matter what. He is 'The Unshakeable' as the baseline of the TV commercial said.

A more recent series of TV commercials for the Sumo Victa features men and women who take on the burden of responsibility, who have their feet firmly planted on the ground, and who will not fail the ones who depend on them.

A couple of years ago, we have seen the campaign for Tata salt, which paid its respect to those who are 'true to their salt' as honest, dependable, upright people.

THE NEVER SAY DIE, WINNER'S ATTITUDE

An article in *Fortune* (issue dated April 4, 2005) about Phil Knight the founder of Nike, recounts that when Knight asked his coach and co-founder of Nike Bill Bowerman, how to improve his running timing, Bowerman said simply: 'Triple your speed'. It is an attitude that runs (no pun intended), right through everything that bears the Nike swoosh, and reflects the will to win.

It is the reason why Nike speaks a language that is in contrast to the language of another era. Whereas the Olympic spirit said that the important thing was not winning but taking part, a Nike advertisement said: You don't win silver. You lose gold.

It is the reason why the headline of another Nike ad said: When your body screams with pain, tell your body to shut up.

It is the reason why Nike appeals to a segment that wants to 'Just do it'.

THE ICONOCLAST

Another hugely appealing and compelling attitude that forms the basis of another one of the world's most iconic brands is the desire to do something original. And we saw the people who took part in the *brandchannel.com* survey, vote it Number One in the Readers' Choice Awards.

As Steve Jobs, the founder of the Apple Computer brand put it, let us 'Make a dent in the universe'. This iconoclasm resonates in *every* phrase of this ad copy from Apple Computer's 'Think different' campaign, and reflects the Apple beliefs, which many people find immensely appealing and which commands a strong loyalty.

> *Here's to the crazy ones...*
> *the misfits...*
> *the rebels...*
> *the troublemakers...*
> *the round pegs in the square holes...*
> *the ones who see things differently.*
> *They're not fond of rules and they have no respect for the status quo.*
> *You can quote them, disagree with them, glorify or vilify them. About the only thing that you can't do is ignore them...*
> *because they change things, they push the human race forward. And while some may see them as the crazy ones, we see genius. Because the people who are crazy enough to think they can change the world...*
> *are the ones who do.*

Think of the other great brands that are not so much about serving needs and offering benefits, but are about an expression of beliefs and attitude. Think of Harley Davidson and how it appeals to a segment of people who respond to a call to walk the wild side.

Think of a brand like *Femina*, which was about the attitude of—and appealed to—the woman who was ready to take on what life had to offer because she was the 'Woman of substance'.

OTHER BASES FOR SEGMENTATION

There maybe yet other ways of defining meaningful segments, which are not specifically described above, and which creatively find links between the product/service and customer groups. Of course they do emerge from the basic areas of demographics, needs & benefits, habits & practices and beliefs & attitudes; but they look at these dimensions in less commonplace ways.

Here are some possibilities, as thought starters:

- o A nightspot can segment the market on the basis of the type of music preferred by guests
- o A readymade garment manufacturer could create a brand for the 'XXL' segment
- o A dessert or ice cream maker could consider catering to a segment defined as diabetes-sufferers

Think about whether there are innovative segmentation strategies you can adopt for your brand. The Action Point chart at the end of the chapter provides a template to carry out your analysis.

Summing Up

In this chapter, the key points to take away are that:

- o *In a world where, a brand trying to be something for everyone, will end up meaning nothing to anyone, the custodians must identify the particular segment of consumers that they will target.*

Segmentation is the process of defining internally homogenous and externally heterogeneous groups that can be reached by customized marketing plans.

- o *If demographically defined sets of consumers who are internally homogenous and externally heterogeneous with reference to the product category and brand exist, this can be the basis of segmentation.*
- o *Second, if there is a specific need or benefit that a section of the population considers more important which can be identified, it can be the basis of segmentation for your brand. However, in highly competitive categories, all the meaningful needs and benefits would probably have been 'claimed' by other brands. A new brand may need to consider a different way of segmenting consumers.*
- o *Another option is to look at differing usage habits and practices as a basis for segmentation. But again, there are only a few usage patterns in any area, and*

> *thus new brands in highly competitive categories will need to find other ways to define target segments.*
> ○ *Perhaps the most useful way to do this is to look at what is happening in the mind and heart of consumers, and segment them by their attitudes and beliefs. Brands which people relate most intimately to, are the ones that share and express a strong view or attitude about some subject. The iconic brands built on such shared beliefs and values attest to the power of this approach.*

Chapter 5: Action Point
Segmentation: Defining the Target Group

Variable to group prospects	Variable 'values' (e.g. 18-25 years) which define a segment	Evidence to support that it is an internally homogenous and externally heterogeneous group
Demographics		
Needs & Benefits Sought		
Usage Characteristics & Practices		
Beliefs/Attitudes		
Any Other Basis		

Understanding Consumers

Why they Buy or Don't Buy

Overview

A little boy woke up crying in the middle of the night, and just would not stop. His father brought him a glass of water, tried to read him a story, even asked him whether he wanted to watch a cartoon on TV…but to no avail. In frustration, he asked his son, 'What do you want?' The little boy replied, 'An earthworm'.

Oh no, thought the father, but the child was still bawling, so he took the child and went out into the garden. He crawled around on his knees in the dark, scratched his hands, got his nails full of dirt, and finally found an earthworm. 'Happy?' he asked his son. Yet the child continued to cry. 'What do you want, now?' asked the father. 'I want you to clean it and cook it,' said the boy. Knowing that the child would not stop until he had his way, the father washed the earthworm, poured a little oil into a pan, and cooked the earthworm; hoping this would finally get the child to stop crying. Not so.

Now close to losing his mind the father asked, 'Now what do you want?' 'I want you to cut it into two bits; then you eat one part and I shall eat the other' said the boy. By now the father was ready to try anything. So he cut the earthworm, picked up one part, closed his eyes and popped it into his mouth. Only to hear the child bawl even more loudly, 'YOU ATE MY PART!!!'

As the story of the difficult-to-please child suggests, it is not easy to satisfy people! More so, when you want them to give you their money! So it is important that you understand how consumers think—why they buy things and why they don't buy things.

In this chapter, we will look at the consumer more closely, and see what are the things that actually keep her from buying brands—that is, the barriers to buying.

Let me begin this chapter by introducing you to my quintessential consumer: Mrs. Gayatri Kulkarni. She is a housewife, 35 years old, a graduate, and mother of two—a son, 11, and a daughter, 8. Mr. Kulkarni, her husband, works as a Production Manager in an engineering company. Mr. Kulkarni's mother also lives with them in their house in Pune. They have a scooter, a refrigerator and an Akai colour TV that they bought through an 'exchange' scheme. They have been working to improve their way of life, and look forward to owning a car some day not too far away. Their entertainment activities are visits to the cinema or eating out; but, more often, a visit to the park or meeting relatives. Mrs. Kulkarni's world largely revolves around looking after her family—especially her children, who are her pride and joy.

Yet, almost imperceptibly, she has changed—and changed significantly—in recent years. Here are some of the changes that have taken place:

- From making sure she cooked good food, now she is also conscious of how she meets her family's nutritional needs and requirements.
- From just keeping expenses within the money available, she now manages the family budget. Including plans for investing their savings, because money saved is money earned.
- From ensuring that her children were looked after, now she looks after their overall development and growth; including their studies, their extra curricular activities and their personal interests.
- From being (just) a mother and wife, she is now a partner and a friend to her children and her husband.
- And she finds ways to fulfill her own individual needs, without neglecting the needs of her family. There is a change in orientation, from a focus on *what she did,* to the *results of her efforts.*

Table 6.1: The changing perspectives of women

Yesterday's Woman What she is (her attributes)	Today's Woman What she wishes to achieve (objectives)
○ Be a good cook	○ Provide an enjoyable meal-time experience
○ Be a good housekeeper	○ Make sure her home looks nice
○ Be there for kids	○ Contribute to the development of her kids
○ Be available	○ Ensure their needs are taken care of
○ Be on 24X7 duty	○ Has her own life, too
○ Be the husband's shadow (*mein unki parchhaayi hoon*)	○ Has her identify (*mera bhi astitva hai*)

Furthermore, with greater exposure to advertising, she has learnt to go a little beyond the face value of advertising claims—perhaps, even become a bit cynical. So, trivial claims and old-fashioned hyperbole don't work as well as they did earlier. If she saw an ad that swore that its product was '*Teen Guna Behetar*' (three times better), she may well ask: *Three times better than what? The ad was only talking of three benefits,* not three ways *in which the product was actually superior to anything!*

This is not to say that all traditional values, beliefs and behaviour have changed; but there are enough changes that are creating a new 'generation' of consumers *every* decade.

Consider some of these changes:

Self-perception among women: The woman is thinking and seeing herself as an individual and seeking an independent income, *even* if she cannot achieve financial independence. This change creates opportunities for women-focused services such as credit cards, insurance policies, and so on.

Personal grooming: Not so long ago, thick, black, long hair was considered a girl's crowning glory (*Kaale, ghane, lambe baal*). Today, most girls wear their hair short and leave it loose. Obviously, this has implications for brands in the shampoo and hair oil categories.

Cooking and Food: While many women are indeed proud of the 'vegetable *makhanwala*' or 'special *sambhar*' that they can dish out, the ability to place great-tasting food on the table for her husband and children may no longer be life's primary aim for others. Simultaneously, many more men are wielding the skillet. What are the implications for ready-to-eat foods? For kitchen appliances? For home-delivery food services?

The fundamental point is that while interest in a particular product—say, a toilet cleaner—may occupy most waking hours of the marketing manager of that toilet cleaner company, it occupies a far smaller part of Mrs. Kulkarni's attention. Because Mrs. Kulkarni has much more to keep herself occupied. And though she may be just *one person, she embodies a host of roles.* Let us look at some of her 'selves shown in Figure 6.1'.

More significantly, these different roles often have competing and conflicting needs and expectations. Take an example of the simple talcum powder. 'Gayatri' (the woman, no surname!) wants the jasmine scented talc she loved from the time she was in college.

Amol's mother thinks the 'cool' talc that can also fight prickly heat is probably best for the family.

Mrs. Abhijit Kulkarni wants to use the expensive, floral talc she knows Mr. Kulkarni loves.

The student at NIIT wants to use a deo-talc which will not only ensure that she'll never feel embarrassed in her class, but will also ensure that she does not appear to be an 'auntie' to all her young class mates there.

Figure 6.1: The many roles Mrs. Kulkarni plays

Sister-in-law to Ashwini, Mr Kulkarni's sister who lives in the US and never lets you forget it	Wife to Mr Kulkarni, friend, homemaker, lover	Mother to Amol and Sonali, arbitrator on arguments, snack food and outings, provider of meals and caring, controller of pocket money, friend
Secretary of her local Ladies club, leader of group, planner of club activities	**Mrs. Kulkarni**	Daughter to Mr & Mrs Joshi. Family counsellor to them and advisor to her younger brother
Student at NIIT course, hardworking, aware that she must not look like an 'auntie' among her young classmates	Gayatri, watcher of old Dev Anand movies, onetime college dramatics star, reader of P. L. Deshpande, ocassional water-colour painter	Friend to her neighbours, confidante, shopping-mate, fellow ice-cream lover, and movie-going buddy

So what do you think she does? It is not so important which one of her 'selves' wins out. What is important is that we think about the question in her mind before she buys that talc: *Where and how will it fit into my life?*

There are a host of inputs that go into answering the question. Some of them are shown in Figure 6.2.

Figure 6.2: Influencers of choice

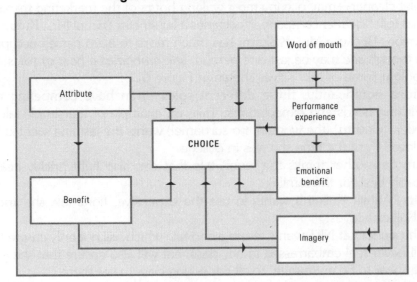

To make matters more complicated, not all these inputs act in a manner that reinforces a particular point of view. Often they are confusing, even contradictory. Yet, because no one likes to live with contradiction, she too, like you, wants a holistic 'fit'. But—and this is a big but—she always has to make trade-offs. To understand this, consider an exercise: *Mrs. Kulkarni and her husband live in the Deccan Gymkhana area, an upper-middle class locality of Pune. As we noted earlier, her family comprises a son, 11, and a daughter, 8; apart from Mr. Kulkarni's mother who also lives with them. After paying taxes, and pay deductions for PF and LIC, Mr. Kulkarni brings home Rs.15500 every month.*

Now, given below is a list of the things that Mrs. Kulkarni needs to run her home. Plan her budget for the month. In fact, the list is not complete—think about what more is needed to manage a home. (I would strongly urge you to carry out this exercise. This, rather than dozens of group discussions or stacks of research reports, will tell you more about how consumers actually have to make choices.)

Mrs. Kulkarni's Shopping list

Item	Quantity	Rate	Total
Rice	6 kg		
Wheat/atta	15 kg		
Tur daal	4 kg		
Moong daal	1 kg		
Whole moong	1.5 kg		
Rajma	1 kg		
Chole	1 kg		
Besan	1 kg		
Cooking oil	4 lts		
Sugar	5 kg		
Tea	1 kg		
Salt	1 kg		
Jaggery	0.5 kg		
Masala	1 packet		
Biscuits	5 packets		

(Contd.)

List (*Contd.*)

Item	Quantity	Rate	Total
Vegetables			
Pickles			
Jam/ketchup			
Eggs/bread			
Toilet soap	4 cakes		
Shampoo 120ml	1 bottle		
Toothpaste 100gms	2		
Hair oil 200ml	1		
Shaving cream/blades			
Woman's cosmetics			
Talc 400gms	1		
Bathroom cleaner	1		
Scouring powder	2 kg		
Detergent powder	2 kg		
Detergent cake	8 cakes		
Floor, toilet cleaner			
Mosquito mats			
Utilities & Services			
Gas			
Rent/society dues			
Electricity			
Transport			
Newspapers, magazines			
Telephone			
Maids			

(*Contd.*)

List (*Contd.*)

Entertainment & leisure			
Cigarettes			
Movies			
Eating out			
Financial			
Home Loan instalment			
Saving			
Children's Expenses			
School fees			
Shoes			
Hair cuts			
Note books, stationery etc			
Mother in law's Expenses			
Medicines			
Doctor's fees			

Not as easy as it looks, is it?

Fact is, Mrs. Kulkarni *has* to make trade offs; she cannot and does not buy just because you want to sell.

Earlier, in attempting to identify sources of business, we saw that consumers may see many products as essentially serving the same need or performing the same basic function. We had also looked at what a girl could do to keep her hair clean.

- o She can, instead of buying your brand, buy a competing brand
- o She can buy another product altogether; such as a soap, which she believes delivers similar performance
- o She can choose to use a service provider, such as a salon
- o She can use a homemade product like *Shikakai*
- o And, in a somewhat extreme option, she can choose to wash hair only with water

What this means is that no one *has* to buy a particular brand, and that they don't even *have to* buy into the branded product category. Actually, we can see that the reasons for not buying—i.e. the barriers to purchase—are of six types.

1. 'WHY SHOULD I BUY IT?'

The most basic barrier, of course, is that the prospect *does not feel the need* for a product. This is a barrier that operates at the product category level itself. Here are some categories where this might be the key barrier:

Microwave oven: Hearsay and misconceptions may exist that these are not suitable for cooking, especially not Indian dishes. If such a perception exists, a prospect may believe that she doesn't need a device that she thinks is basically useful only for re-heating food, and not actually useful for cooking.

Non-stick cookware: A prospect may believe that the major benefit of using these is lower consumption of oil, because less oil is required while cooking in non-stick cookware. However, a prospect may believe that she actually doesn't need the lower consumption of oil promised by this type of cookware, since she has already 'reduced the family's oil intake, by switching to a lighter oil like Soya oil.'

Bottled water: Until not so long ago, most people did not feel that they needed this, because they 'do not fall ill, so why pay for drinking-water?' This has somewhat changed in the recent past, with growing concerns about contamination in water. Bottled water is no longer only the 'Non Resident Indian's (NRI)'s choice.'

2. 'SO WHAT'S DIFFERENT?'

The second barrier—and this one operates at the brand level—is the belief that there is nothing different on offer; and therefore the consumer *feels that he/she is already getting the promised benefit.* Here are some cases where this might be the key barrier.

Branded PCs: These have to compete with locally assembled PCs, thanks to a very simple perception that 'Wintel PCs are, after all, more or less, the same.' Due the strong campaigning by Intel ('Intel Inside') over the years, and the popularity of the Windows operating system; many consumers feel that they *already get the main benefits* a branded PC can offer, in their assembled, Wintel PC.

Eggs: We came across a similar barrier when working on the promotion of eggs for NECC. Some people felt that they did not require the extra nutritive values of eggs because, 'We already get all the nourishment we require.' People who did not include eggs in their diet felt that the specific nutrients that an egg provided already existed in other foods in their diet. In effect, they were already getting the promised benefit.

3. 'IT SOUNDS TOO GOOD TO BE TRUE'

A common barrier is the consumers' natural skepticism about claims by products—regarding their performance or benefit delivery. One reason for this is, obviously, the exaggeration marking the claims made by some brands. Yet, that is by no means the only reason. Here are some cases in which the *barrier is claim credibility.*

Automotive lubricants: Here is a category wherein brands promise better engine performance, longer engine life, improved fuel efficiency, etc. The performance of the engine of a vehicle is affected by many variables including traffic conditions, age of the vehicle, one's driving skills, and so on. It is difficult to isolate the effect on performance of the lubricant. The credibility barrier in this can be: *How will I know if your brand actually delivers the benefit?*

Disinfectants: Floor cleaners, bathroom cleaners and other products which promise disinfectant benefits can run into a claim credibility barrier because the consumer has no way of seeing the 'product at work.' The consumer could not see the germs *before* the product was used, and cannot notice their absence *after* its use!

Preventives: Many products, especially at launch, will face a *credibility barrier, if their benefit is to be realized in the future.* Think of a new product that offers rust-prevention for your vehicle. Or, a skin cream which promises to prevent wrinkles. How would you decide whether the claim was sound? In such cases, the past performance of the brand (in the case of a line extension) or the company becomes critical for credibility.

Variation from experience: It can also be difficult to achieve credibility if some aspect of the brand's action, or performance, seems to be contrary to experience. We have not yet seen communication for dishwashers in India, but I would imagine that prospects would find claims related to 'grease removal' a bit difficult to believe. This is likely because current experience suggests that a fair bit of elbow grease and physical scouring of the surface is necessary to remove grease from utensils that have been used to eat/serve/ prepare many an Indian dish.

4. 'BUT I BELIEVE THAT...'

There are some areas of our lives in which we hold *strong beliefs which can be barriers* to accepting a brand. These may or may not have a scientific basis. For example: 'Debt is the road to ruin.' In the past, the most probable source of a loan was likely to be a local moneylender, who charged usurious rates of interest. It was impossible to pay even the interest, let alone the principal amount; and borrowers would lose everything they owned. The belief quoted above was not invalid in such circumstances. However, it is a belief widely held until quite recently. For some people it is true even today; many old people are wary of taking credit on a card and won't take a loan other than for needs such as housing, education or marriage expenses.

'Eggs are hot for the body, and are to be avoided in summer': There is no evidence that there are deleterious effects of consuming eggs in summer, according to NECC. However, many people believe that eggs do cause heat in the body, and can cause pimples, etc. in summer.

5. 'IT'S NOT WORTH THE PRICE'

Very often, this is the simple barrier to the acceptance of a brand. The owners of the brand, in these cases, overestimate the performance: price ratio that the brand is delivering. Sometimes it is the consequence of overestimating the perceived value of the brand's image; at other times there may be a 'threshold price' barrier to the category. It is important to remember that the ambitions of the brand owners and the economics of the category play a critical role in judging the acceptability of price.

A designer of high-priced formal Indian attire for women might find 100 customers, each one buying, say, 10 pieces per year—a large enough clientele to run a successful boutique. On the other hand, you cannot run a restaurant if you only attract 100 customers who eat there 10 time a year.

Athletic shoes: International brands entered the Indian market with shoes priced above Rs.1500 at the bottom end of the price range. While prospects loved the shoes, the price was clearly more than what they felt the shoes were worth. The brands saw a significant change in acceptance when they introduced shoes for under Rs.1000.

Heinz: It is perceptibly the thickest tomato ketchup available. Yet, it lags behind Kissan and Maggi sauces in terms of market share. For its price, consumers probably do not see an acceptable performance: price ratio.

Ariel, Surf Excel: The price drop—from Rs.85 to Rs.70 per 500 grams— announced by both these brands in mid-2003 was clearly an attempt to arrive at a more acceptable performance: price point.

Automobiles: Several brands introduced models at a particular price, and have then been compelled to reduce them significantly, so as to improve acceptability. Recent examples include the Versa and the Alto cars introduced by Maruti. Some time ago, Daewoo did the same with the Cielo and the Matiz.

6. 'WHERE'S THE BUZZ?'

Finally, a barrier may be the simple fact that a brand has failed to generate a sense of excitement among prospects. Given that most brands do not make for radically different breakthroughs, a sense of anticipation and excitement is critical at launch—in order to avoid the fate of an also-ran. Although 'initial' acceptance/interest does not guarantee long-term success, a brand that fails to generate 'escape velocity' at its launch is unlikely to ever go into orbit.

This is especially so for products in categories such as soft drinks, candy and light snacks where there is no compelling need to try one more offering.

Perhaps the best examples of the value of buzz are to be found in the entertainment business. *Devdas* was the most hyped film in India in 2002. It was the most expensive film ever made in India and, yet, thanks to having become a 'must-see', turned a profit. *The legend of Bhagat Singh* was a far better film, and was less expensively made, but it did not generate the same buzz. It ran into a loss.

Here are some brands which either faded away in recent times, or failed at launch. What, according to you, was the barrier they could not overcome?

- o Mirinda Apple
- o Knorr Annapurna Tiffin
- o Aim toothpaste

Summing Up

The key points to remember from this chapter are:

- o *The consumer may be one person, but she embodies a host of roles. Often, these different roles have competing and conflicting needs and expectations, and the consumer has to make trade-offs between the needs and desires of these selves.*
- o *Second, the consumer receives a variety of inputs, which might influence her choices; to make matters more complicated, not all these inputs act in a manner that reinforces a particular point of view. But because no one likes to live with contradiction she, like you, must make choices that allow her to get a resultant holistic 'fit'.*

○ *Then, of course, there are some specific reasons why the consumer may not choose to buy a brand.*

○ *'Why should I buy it?' The most basic barrier of course, is that the prospect does not feel the need for a product.*

○ *'So what's different?' The second major barrier is born out of the 'me-too' problem: the belief that there is nothing different on offer, and the feeling that he/she already gets the promised benefit.*

○ *'It sounds too good to be true.' Another common barrier is the consumers' natural skepticism about claims by products about their performance or benefit delivery. One reason for this is obviously the exaggeration that marks the claims by some brands. But it could also be that the consumer is unable to find a basis to believe the promise.*

○ *'But I believe that...' Sometimes there may be some areas of our lives in which we hold strong beliefs which can be barriers to accepting a brand or its proposition.*

○ *'It's not worth the price.' Very often, this is the simple barrier to the acceptance of a brand. The owners of a brand overestimate the performance: price ratio that the brand is delivering. Or the absolute price the consumer is willing to pay in that category.*

○ *'Where's the buzz?' Finally, a barrier may be the simple fact that a brand has failed to generate a sense of excitement among prospects, and there is no excitement about wanting to try it.*

Use the Action Point charts to identify the roles of the consumer and the barriers that may be affecting your brand. In the next chapter we will look at how to overcome these barriers.

Chapter 6: Action Point
Analysis of Consumer Roles and Barriers

1. Analysis of Consumer Roles

'Role' played by prospect in relation to category buying	Implication for choice of your brand

2. Analysis of Barriers to Buying Brands

Barrier	Assessment of barrier for your brand
Need perception absent	
Need perceived as already fulfilled	
Brand's ability to deliver questionable	
Deeply held beliefs prevent consideration	
Price: performance acceptability	
Buzz–or its absence	

Motivators and Differentiators

Discovering What can Change the Consumers' Mind

Overview

'Logic gives you what you need, Magic gives you what you want'
    ~Amanda, a character in the Tom Robbins novel, Another Roadside Attraction

We saw in the previous chapter that there are many barriers which may prevent a prospect from 'buying into' a brand or even a product category. Let us now turn to finding out why she does buy the things she buys.

Obviously, a necessary condition is that she believes it fulfills a need, but that is not a sufficient condition for brand preference—which is what we are interested in. In this chapter, we will first look at the factors that get consumers to be interested in a product or brand: these are the motivators.

However, it is not enough for a brand to possess a motivator; after all, if all or several brands in the category can offer the motivator, they will be seen to be no different, For instance, think of the brand of perfume you prefer: several other brands too, might fulfill the same need, but it is likely that you think that there are some aspects of the brand you prefer which go beyond it, and determine your preference.

If in fact you felt that there was no difference between them, the choice would probably be made on the basis of the price. But a power brand must have a basis of preference that goes beyond just a lower price! This factor, which creates a preference for a particular choice, is the differentiator.

If one were to ask Amanda to explain, she would say that brands provide the magic, beyond the functionality of the product, which provides the logic!

In many ways, the brands we use are the 'language and words' that describe what we are. Indeed, we often select the brands we use to say something about ourselves. Here is a little exercise, which is well worth doing. In Table 7.1 are the brands of some products used by three imaginary individuals.

YOU ARE WHAT YOU USE

Table 7.1: Brands as indicators of user personality

	Person A	*Person B*	*Person C*
Drink	Old Monk rum	Royal Challenge whiskey	Officer's Choice whiskey
Preferred dress	Jeans and T-shirt	Formal Trousers and shirt	Safari Suit
Car	Pajero	Baleno	Lancer
Watch	Timex	Titan–Steel	Titan–Gold plated
Soft drink	Thums Up	Limca	Gold Spot

Now, here is the exercise: what do you expect these three individuals to be, considering that all you know about them are the above brand preferences? What would you guess is the age of each person? What would be their likely occupations? What about their favourite leisure activities? Where would they like to go for a holiday? Most importantly, from this information, what would you guess about which brand of readymade shirt each one would be likely to prefer? If you were asked, 'which one of them is most likely to prefer Woodland shoes'; what would your answer be? What about readymade shirts, who is most likely to choose Arrow shirts?

I imagine you would have been able to answer these questions reasonably readily; this is because the above brands in the table have a richness of associations, and help you to draw fairly rich portraits of each one of these hypothetical persons. Just as Woodland and Arrow have fairly well-defined associations.

Now let us try another exercise. In Table 7.2 are the names of brands in different product categories: after shave lotions, motorcycles, and so on. With only the knowledge of the brand used in these categories, try to imagine the SEC, age and education of the typical user of each brand.

You would have seen that it was easier to imagine the user of the different brands of motorcycle or aftershave, than to imagine the users of different brands of cough syrup or ballpoint pens. This is because, quite simply, motorbikes involve more 'magic' and cough syrups involve more 'logic.' Brands in product categories that convey more about what we are, or the way we want others to think of us, have more 'magic.'

Table 7.2: Exercise on brand usage and suggested user characteristics

	SEC	*Age*	*Education*
Deodorant/After shave 　○ Axe			
Motorcycle owned 　○ CBZ 　○ Hero Honda Splendour 　○ TVS Victor			
Ball pen 　○ Luxor 　○ Flair 　○ Cruiser			
Cough syrup 　○ Glycodin 　○ Vicks Formula 44 　○ D'Cold syrup			

When the choice of brands is seen to communicate something about ourselves, we are likely to be more particular about brand choice. Moreover, we are more likely to:

 ○ Have greater brand loyalty towards our preferred brand
 ○ Be willing to pay a price premium for the brand and
 ○ Associate a sense of higher 'perceived penalty of incorrect choice'. In other words, we would be afraid of making the 'inappropriate' choice since it would cue the wrong things about us. (If you have any doubts about the fear of cueing the wrong things due to a choice of brand, try asking for a 'Vimto' the next time you are in a hip restaurant ordering a soft drink!)

BRAND CHOICE AS SELF-REVELATION

However, brand choices in all categories do not cue the personality of the user to the same extent. Figure 7.1 represents four degrees of 'self-revelation' and the kind of product categories that operate at each level.

Level 1: Categories in which the product 'Does what it is supposed to do' would be at Level 1, the orbit furthest from the user's 'core'. A very low-level of self- revelation is involved in these categories, and the brand choice is marginally if at all, linked to the user personality or self-image.

Figure 7.1: Levels of self-revelation and brand choice

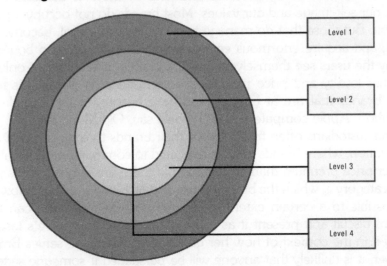

Examples of categories at this level would be: safety pins, scrubbers, floor cleaners, clothespins, handkerchiefs, gas lighters.

Level 2: The choice of brand in the categories at this level provides a sense of 'personal satisfaction.' The degree of self-revelation may still be fairly low, but the brand choice helps to create a sense of feeling good. The type of feel-good effect may be:

- *Personal pleasure* as in the choice of biscuit, tea, toilet soap, etc.
- *Comfort* as in undergarments, shaving razors, etc.
- *Good judgment* as in the selection of health beverage, antiseptic liquid, muscular pain reliever, etc.

Many categories of FMCG and household products belong at this level.

Level 3: Here the brand 'Affects how others see me.' This involves many of the public 'roles' we saw in the previous chapter, and product categories which have a 'badge value' tend to belong at this level.

Categories at Level 3 would include watches, clothes, soft drinks, colognes, mobile phones etc. These are by and large categories in which the brand choice is *visible* to the world.

Level 4: This is the brand owner's Mecca. The choice of brand is almost like making the statement: 'This is me.' At this level, we are speaking of aspects that are intensely personal and help to show or demonstrate our beliefs, our self-image and our values. Most brands do not occupy a place in this orbit. But those that *do* manage to connect at this level, become iconic brands, and acquire enormous equity. In fact they become so bound with the way the users see themselves, that the brands command not only great consumer loyalty and price premia, the users become evangelists for the brand. Brands that are at Level 4 and have become iconic include Nike, Body Shop, Apple computers, and, I would say, Old Monk rum.

Brand custodians often try to 'push' their brands to suggest Level 3 self-identification, where brands may be expected to command more loyalty and a higher price premium than at Level 2, but there are intrinsic limits placed by the category in which the brand operates, which one should acknowledge. It is possible to a certain extent, of course: for example, one can take a brand of biscuit and present it as a reflection of the housewife's tastes, by placing it in the context of how her guests react when she serves Brand X. However, it is unlikely that anyone will be persuaded if someone suggested that the choice of a particular brand of scrubber is going to 'reflect the inner you'!

The reasons why people will choose a product are the motivators a brands must tap in its advertising. But you must also have a differentiator, which sets your brand apart and leads to brand preference.

Great food, drinks and music might be the *motivators* for people to want to attend parties on New Year's Eve. Holding a party on a yacht however, might be the *differentiator,* which will make people want to come to *your* party—rather than the nine other parties they could have gone to!

DIFFERENTIATORS

David Ogilvy's headline for Rolls Royce, 'At 60 miles per hour, the loudest noise in the new Rolls-Royce comes from the electric clock', is possibly the best-known line of copy in English advertising. And it is based on a functional differentiator—the silent running of the engine of a Rolls Royce.

I am old-fashioned enough to believe that the functional difference can be the most important contributor to a brand's success in many more cases than one usually sees. This is especially likely to be so, in categories of FMCG and household products, which are at a Level 2 degree of self-identification.

It is a pity that terms like 'image' advertising and 'lifestyle' advertising have been so misused and abused, that people have tended to forget this factor entirely. To be sure, this is not to suggest that a simplistic level of 'this brand washes clothes whiter' set in Times New Roman makes for great advertising! But it is always a much better idea to have a firm foundation of reality, if possible. And if you believe that 'image' alone can sell, well, all you need to do is think of all the dotcoms, which had great image and no substance—and ask yourself where they are today.

THE SEARCH FOR THE DIFFERENTIATOR

The best place to start your search for functional differentiators is product design. There is a reason why Fiskars uses a specific type of steel. There is a reason why some shoes have removable inner soles. There is a reason why feeding bottles are made from a certain type of plastic. There is a reason why a refrigerator manufacturer uses a certain kind of insulation. There is a reason why a cough syrup has a particular formulation. There is a reason why a product undergoes specific quality control tests before it is sent out of the factory.

In each of these areas of product design, materials, construction, formulation, quality checks, etc. are hidden the potential differentiators your brand can own. You can go about identifying these opportunities in a simple, methodical way.

There are four areas you need to examine. And the best place to begin is probably by talking to the person who designed the product, or with someone who knows the logic behind the design or the formulation. Ask him or her about these areas.

1. Designs & Formulation: Most product categories have evolved over time, with incremental changes, improvements and modifications taking place along the way. Understanding the reasons behind these changes, and the improvements they brought about, offers a potential goldmine of information in which the nuggets of ideas for a differentiator might be found. Consider the following:

- o Design/formulation history of the category. Who invented the product? Where and how was it invented/discovered? Why did the contours of the product change to their current configuration? What is the reason why the way a microwave oven works today is different from the earliest ones? Why are the chemicals used in a lotion today different? Why did quartz watches replace mechanical watches? All such questions help you understand literally, what makes the product category tick.
- o State of the art of the technology: Understand what is the latest international technology or design. Compare it to the state of the art in the country. Why are there differences, if any?

o   Prepare a detailed point-by-point comparison chart of your brand—in terms of the specifications and formulations—with the major brands in the market. Ask the experts the reasons for, and the consequences of, these differences. Ask about differences against other Indian brands and international brands.

Compiling all this information will not be easy; but trying to build a brand without understanding the product itself is like trying to create a garden without bothering to find out what fertiliser, seeds or pesticides are, or what they do!

2. Raw materials/ingredients & sources: This is the second area to be investigated, in terms of raw material specifications and raw material sources.

Raw materials, their source and what they stand for, can add enormous perceived value to a brand. Take away the word 'Dehradun' from a sack of Dehradun Basmati, and you will find that consumers will expect to buy the brand of rice at a lower price. Remove the assurance that it is 'blended with scotch' from the label of an Indian whiskey brand, and you will probably need to reduce the price by Rs100 per bottle to find buyers. Cement made in different parts of the country—even when it is sold under a common brand name—is considered to be of differing quality because of the limestone quality. It is the same reason why a housewife prefers juice made from 'Nagpur oranges', and why pulp from 'Deogadh alphonso' mangoes will sell at a higher price than mango pulp that cannot claim this pedigree.

3. Production Process: The third area that you should investigate is the actual production process and method. The specific aspects you should look at are:

o   Overall process
o   Equipment used, its characteristics
o   Time taken to make the product, or specific stages in the manufacturing process
o   Quality control methods and systems

You can only do this by visiting the factory. You can get great stories out of factories. The details of what makes a Jaguar a Jaguar, why a Paithani saree is valued so much, what goes into the making of a Kashmiri carpet, and so on, can only be discovered by understanding the production process in detail.

4. In-use Characteristics and Packaging: Finally you must understand what the actual performance characteristics of the product are, and what determines the performance. What makes the road-grip of a tyre better? What in the detergent is getting the stains out? Why does a particular kind of bulb last longer? What makes a particular washing machine run more silently? Why is the product packaged the way it is? What would happen if you packed it in tin instead of glass? Does the kind of glass used have any particular characteristics?

And don't be misled into believing this is only true for what you might consider 'technology' products. Not by a long shot. Along with all the 'image' advertising that Nike does, there is a parallel series of communication, which focuses on product innovations and the new shoe technology that lies behind the swoosh. Every great commercial for Levi's, made by Bartle, Bogle, Hegarty; is built around a product feature: the fifth pocket, the riveted pockets, the pre-shrunk fabric, the metal buttons on the fly and so on.

Likewise, you may think of a Lexus as a luxury car and a status symbol, but Lexus advertising is not saying things about its status value, it tells you about how they make it, and what's different in the product and the way they make it.

All of this, of course, would be completely meaningless if it could not be translated into clear consumer benefits, because the thing to note is that *a differentiator must be relevant.* One can attach a shoehorn to a toothbrush and that would be a differentiator in the toothbrush category (or for that matter, in the shoehorn category!). However, since there are not too many people who would see much value in a shoehorn attached to their toothbrushes, it wouldn't be a very useful differentiator.

It is important to be able to convert differences that you identify in the product, into benefits that are relevant to consumers, if they are to be valid differentiators.

While the 'shoehorn attached to a toothbrush' is obviously a wildly fanciful example of an irrelevant 'differentiator', you *will* come across situations where people believe that idiosyncratic, marginal or irrelevant differences are meaningful.

Many years ago, there was a soft drink concentrate called Trinka. The 'differentiator' it offered against Rasna (which was the clear market leader in soft drink concentrates), was that it was a single liquid concentrate which had to be mixed with water and sugar to create the syrup, while the Rasna concentrate was a combination of a liquid and a powder both of which had to be mixed with water and sugar. Does this sound like a major differentiator? Consumers, not surprisingly, did not find it a meaningful differentiator either.

The enzymes in a detergent, which clean with a gentle action, are meaningful differentiators; only if consumers value the fact can get cleaning without damaging the fabric. A six-lever vault lock on a suitcase becomes a meaningful differentiator only if people value the *extra* safety it provides.

How do you tell if the differences you have identified are actually differentiators? There are two old-fashioned, and simple techniques:

1. Find out what consumers say: Talk to current users of the brand. Carry out one-on-ones yourself, attend focus groups, meet real people: your aunt, neighbour, friend, maid, cab driver...A good male obstetrician may never get pregnant, but he has certainly seen a lot of childbirths!

Too many times, brand owners focus their research efforts among people who have never tried the brand, or who have stopped using it. They are hoping to discover what can be done to make their brand appealing to these groups. They ignore a fundamental reality: *you learn more about what people will love in a brand by asking people who love it, not by asking people who don't.*

Think of this example: If you wanted to get more people to come and attend a Bhimsen Joshi classical music concert, what could you offer? And, are you more likely to find out what makes his singing appealing by talking to *his fans* or to people who don't like his singing, and prefer listening to remixes? What use would it be to learn from the latter that they don't like his singing because they like a foot-tapping beat? Are you going to try and get Bhimsen Joshi to sing a Bappi Lahiri number?! Even, assuming for a moment, if you could do it: what do you think will be the effect on his current fans, who love his singing?

By all means, talk to past users, never-triers and other brand (or substitute) users; but you'll get the best learnings from current users.

2. Use the product yourself: Wherever possible, experience the product or service for yourself. Moreover, it is not enough to merely use the product: you need to compare the performance and the experience with competitive products, and with substitutes or alternatives.

For example, if the product you are looking at is a tamarind paste, you need to be able to compare its cooking performance with other tamarind pastes. You also need to compare its performance with the whole tamarind that has traditionally been used in kitchens, to get a sense of the difference in end-taste, convenience, cost and flexibility of usage.

Your perceptions of the relative strengths and weaknesses of the product, of its value in your life, all get sharper. And you get a clearer idea of what can help build a bond between the brand and the consumer. And strengthening that bond is what creating Power advertising is all about.

DEVELOPING THE BRAND PROPOSITION

The *brand proposition is the combination of motivator and differentiator that your brand can offer.* For example, the proposition that the original amber Pears soap offers is: The glycerine soap (differentiator) which helps keep skin from looking 'old' (motivator); and Complan offers to: Help your children in their growing years (motivator) because it has 23 vital nutrients (differentiator). Or consider Bournvita, which will help your child develop stamina and concentration (motivator), because it has the RDA (Required Daily Allowance) of nutrients (differentiator).

Figure 7.2: Press advertisement: Bournvita

Here are some questions which can help you identify the motivator and differentiator that your brand can offer and help you to define your brand proposition.

Is there a perceived compromise that your brand helps consumers to avoid?

For example: Coffee lovers feel that they don't get the *real* coffee taste with instant coffees. Bru coffee used this as a basis to offer differentiation based on 'the taste of real coffee' to customers. The latter could do this because its chicory blend makes coffee taste more like real coffee than 100 per cent instant coffees, such as Nescafe.

Are there usage practices, which you can use as a context, in order to present your brand?

For example: There is a certain segment of people who use an optical whitener such as Ranipal or Robin Blue (there are local brands also available, commonly referred to as *neel*) while washing clothes, to get a really bright white; the perception being that washing powders or detergents alone do not get clothes to be really, really white. Ariel used this very practice as the context in its early launch communication; and went on to offer the kind of whitening power 'that did not need *neel*.'

Is there a specific problem your major competitor/category leader has, which your brand does not?

For example: One of the common problems with washing bars/cakes is that they dissolve easily when left wet/moist. Nirma bar cued in superiority by exploiting the suggestion or perception that the Rin bar dissolves when kept wet.

Is there a 'gold standard' of quality, which you can own?

For example: Oral-B tells you that it is the toothbrush more dentists use— surely that's good enough for most of us! Toothpastes commonly use 'seals of approval' from industry or professional bodies as evidence that they meet the gold standard. Mind you, overuse of this approach in a category devalues the approach itself, as customers begin to see *all products* meeting the gold standard, thus effectively killing it as a differentiator. Unless a new gold standard is established.

Are there any aspects of your brand that makes it particularly suitable for some people?

For example: Vicks Cough Syrup. Since it does not contain alcohol— compared to other cough syrups, which do contain alcohol—many people would feel it is particularly suitable for children. This can be a powerful differentiator, insofar as this segment of users is concerned.

Are there manufacturing or usage characteristics about the product that suggest a desirable difference?

For example: Luxury cars often tell you about the special kind of leather used for the upholstery, or the specially treated wood used for the dashboard. Advertising for suiting fabric often attempts to create differentiation based on the special Merino wool that goes into its making. While whiskey brands talk about the decades of maturing, the special casks, the specially grown ingredients used, and so on—all of which make them the toast of the town!

Is there a generic benefit of the category you can appropriate?

For example: Some times, even taking a characteristic common to most brands in the same category can become a differentiator if a brand can 'own' it. Many years ago, KLM Airlines made a virtue of the numerous rigorous checks that they carried out before each flight. Many or most of these were mandatory checks that *all* airlines carry out; but by 'owning' the notion of meticulous care, KLM could differentiate itself as the 'reliable airline'.

Promise toothpaste made a virtue out of the fact that it had clove oil, and created a perceived differentiation; even though it is a fact that many toothpastes use clove oil in their formulation.

Does the brand have a heritage that can be a differentiator?

Brands in many categories such as wines, whiskeys, watches, etc. draw their uniqueness from a unique heritage. Like, for example, the special processes that may be followed by a winemaker, or fact that Breguet watches use the special hands designed by the man whose name appears on the watch.

REASON WHY, REASON TO BELIEVE

There is one other aspect that you must consider in finalising the proposition. Indeed, in many marketing companies this is considered an essential part of the proposition. You must, of course, give due consideration to whether there is a need for an explicit 'reason to believe' that the brand delivers the promised performance; or that it possesses the stated differentiator.

In the case of Pears soap, for many years, it was the thought that it was a glycerine soap, which was the differentiator. In that case, since it was generally believed that glycerine was good for the skin, there was *no reason* to provide a further 'reason why/reason to believe' the offer of a young complexion.

Similarly, in the case of Complan, it is the '23 vital foods' that makes for the differentiator; and supports the promise of promoting growth. Here, there is no need for 'a second-level' reason why/reason to believe whether there actually are 23 vital foods in Complan; or to provide a separate 'reason why/reason to believe' that the 23 vital foods actually help growth.

Where consumers have knowledge or belief about the properties of some ingredients or the way in which a product works, or the reputation of a company is strong, they do not need further 'reason' to believe the claim. If consumers generally believe that *shikakai* is good for the hair, it is enough for you to tell them that your shampoo has *shikakai*—you need not give reasons to believe why *shikakai* is good for the hair. If people believe that fluoride is good for teeth, it is enough to say your toothpaste has fluoride. There is no reason to gild the lily.

Also remember that the customer is not necessarily looking for a 'relentless and inevitable chain of proof' when deciding which brand to buy. There is no need to spell out *every* step of the logic, as shown here:

4. *Keeps teeth healthier*

↑

3. So you can *trust us* when we say it...

↑

2. That XYZ toothpaste *prevents cavities*...

↑

1. It is *certified* by ABC institute...

The prospect is not going to disbelieve you if you collapsed this to:

2. XYZ toothpaste *keeps teeth healthier*

↑

1. *Certification* by the ABS institute is evidence that...

The consumer is only a buyer of toothpaste, not a judge in a courtroom following *every* step of a relentless logic! (If your discriminator/reason-to-believe is not supported by adequate facts, a marketer may find himself talking to another kind of judge, but that is not likely to happen to you, is it?!)

However, *when the prospect is not familiar* with the properties of a critical or the differentiating ingredient, it is necessary to explain why it is good for someone or does what you say it will do. So, in the early years when fluoride toothpastes were launched, it was necessary for brands of toothpaste with fluoride to explain to customers what exactly fluoride did, and how it helped to have fluoride in a toothpaste.

It is also useful to remember that your task becomes far simpler if you can ride on an existing belief or perception, rather than if you are attempting to establish one. It makes things even more difficult when you are trying to say something that runs contrary to what people widely believe—even if the belief is incorrect. For example, if a brand of ceiling fan were to say it 'has roller ball bearings', this would make sense only if the prospect had some notion of why roller ball bearings are good things to have in a fan! Brand owners sometimes get carried away into believing that the lay public is familiar with norms and terms; which, in fact, are jargon that only industry insiders know.

However, as competition increases, it is likely that yesterday's differentiator becomes today's 'fundamental characteristic'. So fluoride in toothpastes has become a basic ingredient of toothpastes in some markets. Conditioners in shampoos, which were a differentiator in the 80s, are more or less table stakes in all shampoos today. Similarly, sun-blocking ability or UV protection is becoming a basic property of skin creams and lotions.

Product categories in which technology development is rapid—such as computers and telephony—are particularly vulnerable to this phenomenon. Take computers, hard-disk storage; the computing power of the chips used, and the capabilities of the operating system are continually being redefined. Barely has the prospect been thrilled by the possibility of 40 GB storage, when along comes a brand which gives 80 GB as the 'minimum' level storage, and redefines the norm.

In mobile phone services, SMS, multimedia messaging, email, cricket scores, share price information, and customized ring tones have all followed in rapid succession as mobile telephone brands attempt to define the 'next level' of services.

In Internet-based email services like Hotmail, Lycos, G-mail and Yahoo; we have seen the incorporation of free spam-protection as well as virus–detecting features. And, more recently, even humungous inbox capacities of 1 GB, came in as differentiators only to rapidly become commonplace in the category.

PROPOSITIONS THAT OVERCOME BARRIERS

In closing, let us consider how the brands that we looked at in the previous chapter overcame the barriers they faced.

1. BARRIER: 'WHY SHOULD I BUY IT?'

As we saw, one of the main barriers to the use of bottled water was that people simply did not see any need or use for it, since they felt, 'we are not falling ill, so why do we need to pay for drinking water?' Kinley, the brand of bottled water launched by Coca Cola, addressed this barrier. In their communication, the company pointed out *the danger of infection and illness for small children*, also including the advice of an expert. Even adults, who do not feel that they need pure water, are likely to believe that they must protect their children as much as possible. Hence, what is considered a barrier in one context is overcome by presenting the brand in another context.

2. BARRIER: 'SO WHAT'S DIFFERENT?'

This is another way of saying, 'I already get the benefits'. In case of NECC, we saw how some people felt that they did not require the extra nutritive values of eggs because they believed, 'we already get all the nourishment we require'. Many people felt that the specific nutrients that an egg provided were already present in other foods in their diet; and, therefore, did not see the reason to include eggs in their diet. The way we, at Enterprise Advertising, overcame this barrier in the communication developed for NECC, was by talking about *the needs of persons who needed more than the 'average' level of nutrition* in their diet. Women agreed that during pregnancy and when they were breast-feeding an infant, they *needed* more nutrition than at other times. In effect, they agreed that they needed nutritional supplementation to their diet. For them, the argument that 'I already get the benefits' did not ring true, and they could see the value of adding eggs to their regular diet (see Figure 7.3).

3. BARRIER: 'IT SOUNDS TOO GOOD TO BE TRUE'

This is a polite way of saying, 'I don't believe you'. In the automotive lubricants category, brands promise better engine performance, or longer engine life, or improved fuel efficiency and so on. The performance of the engine of a vehicle is affected by many variables including traffic conditions, age of vehicle, driving skills etc., and it is difficult to isolate the effect of the lubricant on the performance of the vehicle. The prospect cannot be blamed for asking: *how will I judge if your brand actually delivers the benefit?* Castrol used endorsements from car and motorcycle racing professionals to support their claim of Castrol delivering superior engine performance. The credibility of the spokesperson becomes the surrogate for the credibility of the claim. If you feel that people may not believe a claim made by the brand itself, you may be able to overcome the credibility gap by finding someone whom they trust, to convey the message.

One of the dangers in using the endorsement route to overcome this barrier is, of course, that the endorser himself/herself may not be seen as

Figure 7.3: Press advertisement: NECC, for pregnant women

having any claim credibility. This danger is all the more when the endorser used is someone who is seen as endorsing anything with a price tag! The endorser can, then, lose credibility; and the entire purpose of using the celebrity to make the claim credible is defeated.

4. BARRIER: 'BUT I BELIEVE THAT...'

There are some areas of our lives wherein we hold *strong beliefs that can be barriers* to accepting a brand. We saw that one of these relates to the belief which many people have: 'Debt is the road to ruin.'

Citibank Silver Credit cards *used an even stronger belief, to overcome this belief barrier.* It presented its Citibank Silver Credit Card as a means to buy the computer that would, in turn, *help the cardholder's child* in his/her studies. Since the belief that one must do the best one can to equip

Figure 7.4: TV commercial: Citibank credit cards

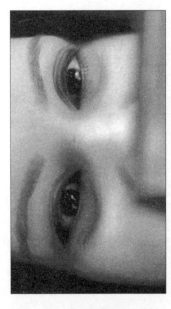

...Cash *bina kharidne ki azaadi mil gayi.*" A girl's eyes light up as she surveys herself in the mirror.

Another family's purchasing power is enhanced by the Citybank Silver Card. Their son is all excited about the...

A couple walks out of a store with the things they wanted to buy. Jingle: "*Ab to zindagi khush haal ho gayi...*

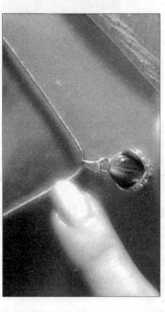

She has a beautifully crafted pendant adorning her neck—a gift from her boyfriend.

All these people can spend without having to think twice as "Citibank Silver Card *liya to chandi ho gayi.*"

...computer he gets. And in a clothes store, a wife lovingly tries out a kurta on her husband.

... the card's features. Super: Citibank, where money lives.

People all over enjoy this freedom to spend as the super highlights...

one's child for the future, is among those strongly held by parents, they may be willing to overcome a 'lower-order belief' in order to satisfy a 'higher-order' belief.

To overcome barriers created by a strong belief, one may explore what could be the *Maximum Utility Value* the product/service can deliver. This often takes the form of shifting the perceived benefits from the individual, who holds the belief, to others such as family members who stand to benefit.

5. BARRIER: 'IT'S NOT WORTH THE PRICE'

This is a simple case of operating at meaningful Price–Performance points. Of course the notion of 'meaningful' involves a consideration of the volumes you can get, or the number of customers you can attract at that price point. There is no point in operating at a price point where too few people perceive a worthwhile Price–Performance being delivered.

The price-drop from Rs.85 to Rs.70, per 500 gram, announced by Ariel and Surf Excel during mid-2003, was clearly an attempt to arrive at a more acceptable performance: price point for a much larger user population.

6. BARRIER: 'WHERE'S THE BUZZ?'

And finally, in a world of consumers jaded by new brands, new products and an overdose of media hype, the arrival of yet another widget, soap, car—or whatever—is often received with a resounding 'ho-hum' expression of boredom.

A powerful mechanism to overcome this is the creation of anticipation and excitement around the brand. Admittedly, this is a tactical rather than a strategic initiative; but one might say that if the brand has failed to generate interest at launch, there may be nothing left to strategise about!

As industries go, it is perhaps the entertainment industry that has used this most successfully. Even here, there are the masters: Steven Speilberg, George Lucas, and the Wachowski brothers with *The Matrix* and its sequels in Hollywood. In India, too, Ram Gopal Varma today, and Raj Kapoor from an earlier generation are examples of film marketers who are masters at creating anticipation for their films.

Yet, the power of 'buzz' has been harnessed by other industries too. A modern-day master, who has perfected it into an art, is Sir Richard Branson. He has launched airlines, music companies, a soft drink, a cellular phone service, and other businesses with unparalleled buzz. (So much that sometimes one wonders if it is the Branson brand or the Virgin brand, which is selling!)

Figure 7.5: Poster: *Darna Mana Hai*

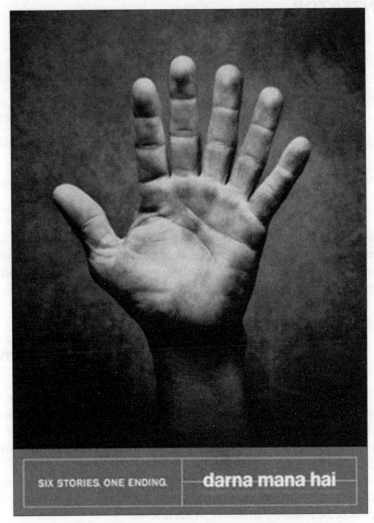

Courtesy: Ram Gopal Varma/Varma Corporation

A mapping of possible motivators and differentiators for your brand, is an exercise you must carry out. Some examples are shown below.

For example: if you were marketing a brand of luggage, you may begin by considering the locking system as a parameter. A sample chart (Table 7.3) shows how this may, in turn, lead to identifying a motivator and a differentiator. You may also want to consider whether the parameter termed as 'packing compartments' works for you. Or, if the 'wheel arrangements' do…you may recall how a recent offer from VIP luggage focused on the capability of one of its luggage models to turn 360 degrees.

IDENTIFICATION OF THE MOTIVATOR AND DIFFERENTIATOR

Table 7.3: Examples of motivators and differentiators

Category & Parameter	Motivator Opportunity	Differentiation Opportunity
Luggage; Lock	Superior safety	6-lever vault lock vs the normal 4-lever lock
Undergarments; Fabric	Fabric will not 'sag'	Fabric with 'Spandex' vs ordinary cotton
Car battery: Warranty	Worry-free driving	3-year warranty vs usual 1-year warranty

Look carefully at the various aspects of the product, its features, and its performance characteristics, to see where you can identify differentiators and motivators. Then, evaluate them to see which ones are most compelling.

Additionally, ask yourself the stimuli questions to get your imagination going!

Summing Up

The key points to remember from this chapter are:

○ *When the choice of brands is seen to communicate something about ourselves, we are likely to be more particular about brand choice. Moreover, we are more likely to have greater brand loyalty towards our preferred brand and be willing to pay a price premium for it.*

○ *However, brand choices in different categories do not cue the user personality to the same extent. We can think of four levels of 'self-revelation' and the kind of product categories involved at each level.*

○ *At Level 1 are categories in which the product 'Does what it is supposed to do' such as: safety pins, scrubbers, floor cleaners, clothespins, handkerchiefs, gas lighters.*

○ *Level 2 categories provide a sense of 'personal satisfaction' and a sense of feeling good. The type of feel-good effect may be:*

    – *Personal pleasure as in the choice of biscuit, tea, toilet soap, etc.*

    – *Comfort as in undergarments, shaving razors, etc.*

    – *Good judgment as in the selection of health beverage, antiseptic liquid, muscular pain reliever, etc.*

○ *Many categories of FMCG and household products belong at this level.*

○ *At Level 3 the brand 'Affects how others see me.' This includes product categories that are visible to the world and which have a 'badge value' such as watches, clothes, soft drinks, colognes, mobile phones etc.*

○ *Finally, at Level 4 are the iconic 'This is me' brands that help to show our beliefs, our self-image and our values. Brands which are at Level 4 and have become iconic include Nike, Body Shop and Apple computers.*

○ *We saw that the reasons why people will choose a product are the motivators a brands must tap in its advertising. But you must also have a differentiator, which sets your brand apart and leads to brand preference.*

○ *The areas of product design, materials, construction, formulation, quality checks, etc. are all potential areas where you can find the differentiator your brand can own.*

○ *Finally, we noted that you learn more about what people will love in a brand by asking people who love it, not by asking people who don't. The understanding of the relative strengths and weaknesses of the product, and of its value in your life, help to develop the brand proposition i.e. the combination of motivator and differentiator that your brand can offer.*

○ *The stimuli questions and the consideration of parameters as shown in the Action Point charts will help you to identify the motivator and discriminator for your brand.*

Chapter 7: Action Point
Discovering What Can Change the Consumers' Mind–1

Motivator and Differentiator Identification: Work Chart

Parameter	Motivator Opportunity	Differentiation Opportunity

Chapter 7: Action Point
Discovering What Can Change the Consumers' Mind–2

Motivator and Differentiator Identification

Stimulus Question	Differentiator	Motivator	Proposition Statement
Is there a perceived compromise that your brand helps consumers to avoid?			
Are there current usage practices that you can use as a context, in order to present your brand?			
Is there a specific problem your major competitor/category leader has, which your brand does not?			
Is there a 'gold standard' of quality that you can own?			
Are there any aspects of your brand that makes it particularly suitable for some people?			
Is there any generic benefit of the category you can appropriate?			
Does the brand have a heritage that can be a differentiator?			

CHAPTER 8

Positioning

Identifying what can make your Brand Unique

Overview

Isadora Duncan, the celebrated dancer, is supposed to have said to George Bernard Shaw, 'How wonderful our child could be—with my looks and your brains!' G.B. Shaw, the pragmatist, apparently answered, 'But what, if the child has my looks and your brains, my dear!'

It is amazing how the entire meaning and inference changes when you look at something from a different perspective. One of the tasks of advertising is to 'direct' the receiver of a message to look at a brand from a perspective: this is what positioning does—it gets people to look at it from an angle which highlights what is most desirable and competitive about it. Isadora Duncan, in the story we just looked at, was looking at herself along the 'beauty' angle. G.B. Shaw, on the other hand, was looking at her along the 'brains' dimension!

There have been references to positioning in earlier chapters, but we had noted that the concept of positioning is important enough to be looked at separately. In this chapter we will begin by going back to the basics of the idea of positioning. It is useful to do this because the term is used so widely that one can be tempted to believe one knows what it means—until we take a closer look!

We shall then look at the different ways in which brands can be positioned, and consider examples of brands which have used different positioning approaches. This will give the reader an understanding of the different situations in which to use them.

Positioning as a concept is too widely used, to be excluded from a book on advertising planning.

The Positioning concept gained the attention of marketers and advertising professionals and has continued to be widely used because it suggested a way to differentiate brands, when they found it difficult to offer product or benefit-based differences.

Here is how Al Ries (who, along with Jack Trout, wrote *Positioning: The battle for your mind*, the original book on positioning), puts it: Positioning is not what you do to the product; it's what you do to the mind of the prospect. It's how you differentiate the brand in the mind...*Positioning focuses on the perceptions of the prospect not the reality of the brand.*
~As quoted by Laura Reis on *http://ries.typepad.com/ries_blog*

(The author has added *italics* to the above quotation to emphasise a critical aspect of the positioning concept: that it has more to do with how the consumer thinks about the brand rather than whether that thinking is related to some specific 'reality' of the brand.)

Let us take an example to understand this. The car brand Volvo is positioned as 'the safer car'; which means that the consumer perceives it as providing greater safety. The point about positioning is that it is this perception among consumers that is important; not whether, in reality, a Volvo is a safer car.

The other thing to note is that there are two 'ends' to the positioning effort: the intention of the marketer, and the result achieved. This is also an important thing to remember. The actual position a brand achieves or occupies is not the one intended by the marketer, but the perception that finally exists in the mind of the consumer. And, this resultant perception is impacted by many factors.

Here, I would like to point out an important reality check you must carry out about the position your brand can potentially occupy. This is because the reality of the brand places limits on what can be achieved. So, although the focus of positioning is perceptions—and not the reality of the brand—the perceptions of the prospect cannot be *entirely* dissociated from the reality. Thus, while you may *want and will probably succeed* in positioning the Ambassador car as the 'Travel-anywhere car', you are unlikely to succeed in positioning it as 'The sporty car'—the intended position is simply too far removed from the reality of the brand!

If the exercise in Chapter 7 has yielded powerful differentiators, they may directly lead to positioning ideas. However, the concept of positioning requires you to reduce the idea to a simplicity, which the consumers will recall easily—because, in an overcrowded market and an over-communicated society, they will not take the trouble to remember complex or detailed messages.

Yet—and this is very important—it implies that you have to make a choice. You have to decide what is the single thing you want the brand to be known for. In spite of all the rhetorical homage paid to the idea of being single-minded, it is here that you will be most tempted to add 'secondary' benefits, ideas, etc. to the brand. Consider these choices:

○ Should Vicks Cough Syrup be 'The children's cough syrup' or 'The no-drowsiness cough syrup'?

    ○ Should Complan be 'The complete nutrient provider' or 'The growth builder'?

    ○ Think about which of these (or other possibilities) would you bet on for these brands. And why?

Listed in Table 8.1 are the most trusted brands in India according to a survey conducted. Ask yourself: What is the 'position' occupied by each of these in the consumer's mind? Do they all have a *clear position*? How distinctive is the position?

Many of these, like Ponds or Britannia, are 'mother brands' with a slew of products under them. All the more reason to ask whether they can be said to have a clear position i.e. is there a common thread running across these products that bear the brand name?

Table 8.1: India's ten most trusted brands

India's Most Trusted Brands	
1	Colgate
2	Dettol
3	Pond's
4	Lux
5	Pepsodent
6	Tata Salt
7	Britannia
8	Rin
9	Surf
10	Close-up

Source: 'Brand Equity', *The Economic Times*, 17 December 2003)

BACK TO BASICS

Before we go into further detail on positioning, consider the following statements about some well-known brands:

    ○ Close-Up is positioned for urban youth
    ○ Godrej Hair Colour is positioned for trendy Indian women
    ○ Jet Airways is positioned for business travellers
    ○ Indian Airlines packages are positioned for holiday-travellers

Notice anything odd about these sentences? Think about it for a minute…

Figure 8.1: Press advertisement: Indian Airlines holiday packages

The point to note about all these sentences, is that they reflect some confusion between 'positioning' and 'segmentation.' Let us put these concepts together to see the difference.

Segmentation is the process of *defining internally homogenous and externally heterogeneous groups* that can be reached by customized marketing plans.

Positioning is the process of *managing how consumers see your brand* in relation to competitive offers.

Do you appreciate how these truncated definitions show the difference? Segmentation refers to the group of people you want to cater to, while Positioning refers to how brands are perceived. A rough rule of thumb to check whether a statement reflects segmentation, is to ask yourself if it uses the phrase 'for (such and such) people'? If it does, it probably refers to segmentation. (It *is* possible to position a brand in relation to a user group, but it only works in certain circumstances. We shall look at this later in the chapter.)

The Close-Up statement refers to the 'youth' segment. The Godrej Hair Colour statement refers to the 'modern Indian woman' segment. The Jet Airways statement refers to the 'business traveler' segment.

We saw that the earlier statements were really *about target segments*, not about positioning. Here is how we would describe the brands in terms of *positioning* statements:

- ○ *Close-Up:* The *fresh breath toothpaste.*
- ○ *Godrej Hair Colour:* The *hair colour specially formulated for Indian hair.*
- ○ *Jet Airways:* The *airline* that *makes flying a joy.*

We can use these examples to define a second thumb rule to look at positioning. The above statements are in the following form: The _____ (differentiator) _____ (product category or competitor)

Thus we say:

Close-Up: The fresh breath (differentiator) toothpaste (product category).

The statement can also be written in another form:

The _____ (product category) with/for/that _____ (differentiator)

This is what we did when we said:

Godrej Hair Colour: The hair colour (product category) specially formulated for Indian hair (differentiator).

Jet Airways: The airline (product category) that makes flying a joy (differentiator).

If you can write statements about a brand in these forms, you are describing the positioning of the brand!

It is important to note that while there is usually a segmentation decision *implicit* in a positioning strategy, the degree of 'fit' between the two may vary significantly.

For example, the *fresh breath* position of Close-Up might possibly be more relevant to the youth, but it is not *intrinsically* linked to this segment i.e. it does not exclude other segments. In another example from the toothpaste category, one may assume that the danger of tooth decay is higher among children; but Pepsodent has taken its 'continues to fight decay after brushing' position to adults in one of the commercials from its *'dhishum dhishum'* campaign. The TV commercial features a sports coach who is advised by a young student about the value of a toothpaste which has a longer lasting effect; and does not leave the viewer with any sense of 'mismatch' between the 'continues to fight decay after brushing' position and the adult user.

Similarly, while young trendy women may be a large set of hair colour users, there is nothing in the 'suited for Indian hair' position of Godrej Hair Colour that is intrinsically locked into this segment.

However, the concepts of segmentation and positioning *are* closely related, and you should take a decision on the segment you are targeting, before you get down to the task of defining the position you want your brand to occupy.

Positioning is a concept most useful in competitive markets and helps you build strong bonds with a specific set of consumers i.e. *the segment* you have decided to address, even if that means giving up other consumers. In fact, powerful positioning is as much about deciding what to forgo, as it is about choosing the area on which to focus your efforts.

Let us consider some examples.

Figure 8.2: TV commercial: Pears soap

Mother and daughter...

...are playing

The mother smiles enigmatically as she locks eyes with her little girl.

MVO: *Subah ki kirnon se sparsh our kahan?* A bar of Pears soap plays hide and seek with the clouds.

...Baarish ki pehli boondon se sparsh. Aur kahan?

...Shudh sparsh. Shudh Pears.
Super: 'Pears, Pure & gentle.'

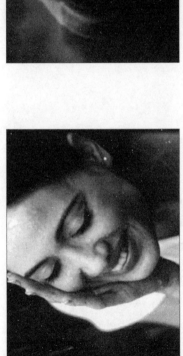

The woman plays with the splattering raindrops as the MVO continues...

The girl feels her mother's cheeks, Aisi Pears twacha aur kahan?

Think of Pears and Cinthol. These two soaps make two very different promises and are positioned very differently. Neither one can fit comfortably in the arena occupied by the other. In other words, Pears has *given up* possible associations with freshness and confidence and the prevention of body odour, in order to build a strong youthful-complexion position.

Cinthol, on the other hand, focuses on how it helps avoid body odour and gives you the confidence to get close to people. Cinthol has *given up* the complexion care area in order to build a freshness and confidence position. In competitive categories, a brand simply cannot be all things to all people.

Or, take specialty petrol. Speed from Bharat Petroleum offers speed, while Xtra Premium from Indian Oil is positioned as 'the best your vehicle can get'.

Figure 8.3: Press advertisement: Xtra Premium from Indian Oil

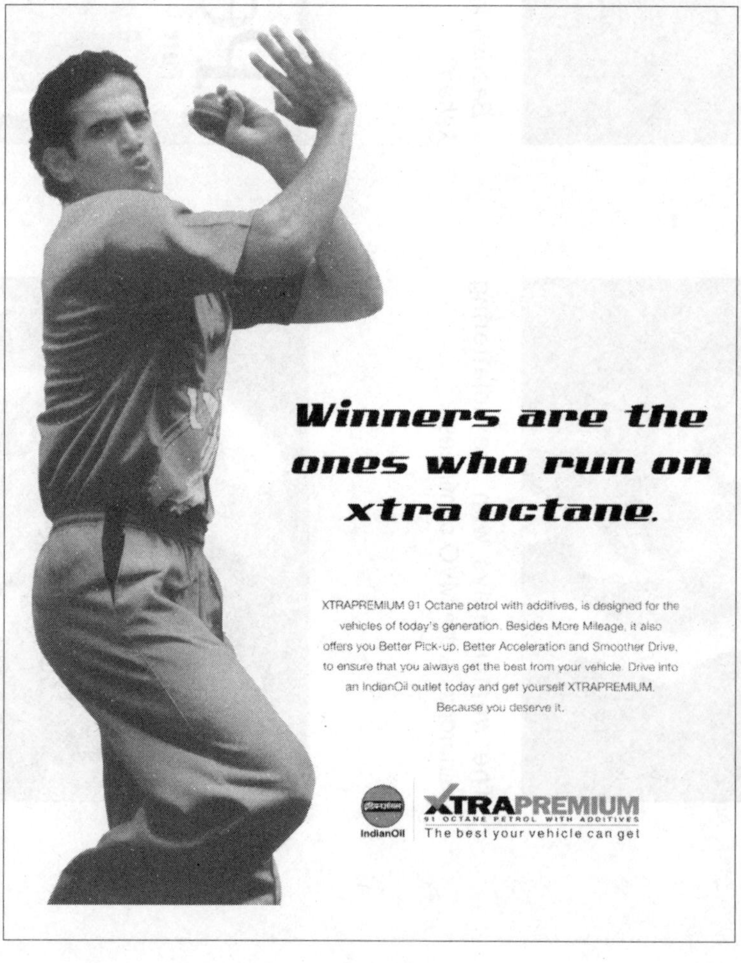

In these cases, the type of person to whom the position will appeal is not very clear (apart from the self-referencing characteristic such as Pears appealing to slightly older women for whom a youthful complexion is important).

There are, however, other cases, where the segment being targeted is intrinsically and strongly linked to the position. Brands that achieve this 'fit', and thus almost *exclude some segments*, are able to create much stronger bonds with their consumers.

Consider just a couple of examples.

MTV is clearly targeting the youth segment. However, the segmentation is not what makes it unique. After all, there are *many* other brands that use music, films, trendy VJs just as much as MTV and all of them, target youth. The key difference is that MTV is the only one with a clear position: The cheerfully irreverent television channel.

Or, take the example of Johnson & Johnson in baby care products. The fact that they are created for the baby segment, *plus* the 'safe and gentle' position that Johnson & Johnson products occupy, are inextricably bound, are what makes the brand so strong. Not surprisingly, this strength is reflected in the price premium these products command.

But, let us return to the concept of positioning.

The very word 'position' relates to a 'location'; as in the phrase, 'the fielder was positioned at mid-on.' If the position or location is to have any meaning, it must be defined in relation to a meaningful axis. On the cricket field, the line that bisects the ground along the pitch defines the primary axis, and its ends are defined by the location of the batsman and the bowler. Hence the positions, 'mid-on' and 'mid-off' (with due adjustment for whether the batsman is a right or a left-hander of course!); or, 'mid-wicket' and 'cover.' The point to note is that if you did not have a pitch or had not defined the ends, you could not have a point defined as 'extra cover'—it would simply have no *locus standi!* The same is true of attempting to describe brand positions.

On a cricket pitch, the fundamental axis of the pitch and the end points are adequate to define all the 'positions', which players occupy. In the brand-space, there are potentially many more axes, but even here, there are only a few axes that are meaningful!

POSITIONING AXIS 1: PRODUCT CATEGORY

At the broadest level of identifying competition, a brand can position itself with reference to an entire product category. This is a strategy, which works in two kinds of scenarios.

The first is when a product innovation is involved. In such a situation, if there is a sufficient discontinuity being brought about by the brand, the consumer has no clear basis of comparison to evaluate the new product. Advertising can help to provide this reference point by referring to an entire product category. Al Reis and Trout have used the example of how the early trains were known as the 'Iron Horse'. Even the Indian Postal Service uses the term 'Speed Post' to describe their express service, positioning it against ordinary post.

There is an interesting example concerning cameras that illustrates the point about *which reference point to use* for positioning, quite dramatically.

A marketer, who had studied the market for cameras, felt that there was a potentially large market for low-priced cameras; particularly among people who used or needed them infrequently. He figured that such people would like a really inexpensive camera; in fact a camera so inexpensive that they could actually dispose it off after use, just as people use disposable cigarette lighters and disposable ball-point pens. He developed such a 'throw-away' camera with a built-in film, which cost only a fraction of the price of a regular camera. The buyer could click the usual 24 or 36 frames; then hand the whole thing over to the processor and get the photographic prints.

Here was a discontinuous, innovative product which was positioned with reference to the camera category as a 'throw-away' camera.

Yet there is also an important lesson in this example, about *the product category against which to position your product*: because, although it was a wonderfully innovative product, there were few takers for this 'throw-away' camera. The reason for this was that most people thought of the very concept of a 'camera' as a precision-engineered, quality product that you used over many years. The idea of throwing away a camera made people feel somewhat guilty.

The company found a way out of this with an interesting solution: they changed the reference product category. In the revised strategy, *the product was positioned against films instead of cameras*. Instead of being called a 'throw-away camera' the product was called a 'smart film.' Now it was a *film that didn't need a camera, instead of being a camera that you threw away after one-time use*—and it cost only twice as much as ordinary film! It was able to overcome the earlier consumer resistance to a significant extent.

The second scenario, when one can position a brand against a category, is when a brand can serve a particular need being served by a single large brand, or a generic product.

An example of positioning against a category, in such a scenario, was the launch of Crowning Glory by Godrej some years ago. It was soap, but developed on the basis of the fact that many people used their toilet soap to also wash their hair. It thus promised luxurious, thick hair, while it was obviously going to be used as toilet soap too! Here then, was a soap positioned against the shampoo category. (It is interesting to note that Shikakai soaps, which are, essentially, hair care products, in a solid form, are also used in the same way. Yet since Shikakai has strong hair-care credentials, its soaps have survived; while Crowning Glory, which did not have these credentials, has not.)

However, it must be noted that such positioning against a product category works best as long as the brand in question remains an innovative product; and is different from most of the products performing a comparable function. Once competition in the new 'product-type' grows, and a new category or sub-category gets established, this strategy is not enough: brands must then *find positions with reference to each other.* Thus, once several courier companies are in operation, the positioning against postal services becomes invalid and they must find positions with reference to each other.

It is useful in this discussion to digress a bit for a moment and discuss positioning against a specific competitor. The most discussed example of this strategy is probably the Avis 'we're number 2, we try harder' positioning against Hertz. It is important to note that very few brands actually displace a leader with such an approach. However, the approach *does* reduce the 'comparison set' by effectively conveying, 'I am in the same league as the leader'. It is the strategy you will see adopted by unknown starlets in the film industry, who proclaim, 'I am not competing with Kareena Kapoor (or whoever the leading star might be at that point)'. Well, the fact might be that *no one* believes the starlet is competing with Kareena, but at least the statement gets her name mentioned along with Kareena's!

POSITIONING AXIS 2: TARGET GROUP

Earlier in the chapter, we looked at the confusion that occurs sometimes between positioning and segmentation. Any positioning based *only* on identification with a target segment, is likely to prove weak in the context of competitive actions.

Also, the success of opening up a new segment invites competitors to target the same segment and thus, almost paradoxically, the very success of a target group based positioning by a pioneer brand brings about an elimination of the uniqueness of the pioneer's targeting strategy.

However, this can be a strong axis for positioning if there are no other brands serving a particular niche target group. For this reason, the target group based approach works better in cases where the target is defined in other than merely demographic terms.

Smokers' toothpaste is an example of positioning based on a specific target group: smokers. By the very nature of this group, such a positioning is likely to create preference among them, over 'general' toothpastes. As a long-term strategy this approach is best when the brand is addressing a relatively small, niche market, where a strong first-mover advantage along with the relatively small size of the opportunity, works as an entry barrier to competing brands.

We noted earlier that MTV is the only youth/music channel that has a clear position, of the cheerfully irreverent television channel.

Yet, because cheerful irreverence is so intrinsically a characteristic that youth relate to, the MTV brand is the youth channel. It is this aspect that has led to the amazingly strong bond that MTV has established with its viewers. After all, how many brands have given their name to an entire generation of people as in 'the MTV generation'?

It allows MTV to be more than just an 'entertainment' partner to youth. The strong association which MTV has established, allows the MTV brand to involve itself with the lives and concerns of young people such as their concern about AIDS, and their icons.

Figure 8.4: Poster: MTV Youth Icon

POSITIONING AXIS 3: USAGE PATTERNS

There are some categories wherein, by definition, there are limited variations in time or manner of usage. How much variation is there in the manner of using a floor cleaner?

Yet, there are several categories where the time and manner of usage can offer opportunity for establishing a position. Among the categories, with greatest variation possibilities, are categories in the food business. You could presumably serve almost any biscuit with tea, but it was Britannia Marie that established a strong position for itself as the 'Teatime biscuit'.

Maggi Noodles has established a position as the 'filling snack in-between-meals.' This bears a moment's discussion: although Maggi Noodles was launched as the '2-minute noodle', its positioning is *not* based on the '2-minute' aspect. If it *were*, Maggi Noodles would be in competition with the '2-minute sandwich' and the '30-second banana' and the '1-minute biscuit pack.' Mothers think of it as a filling snack, and the convenience is merely a trinket on the Christmas tree (as an aside, it is perhaps akin to the 'reason' a businessman I know once gave me for buying a Mercedes; 'Of course it has its status value', he said dismissing it as the reason for buying it, 'but I like the fact that with a diesel engine, it is more economical on fuel-cost than a petrol car!')

Milkmaid's condensed milk was repositioned on the manner of usage dimension—from a 'milk substitute' position, to the position of 'ingredient for sweet dishes'.

What other examples of positioning based on time or manner of usage can you think of?

POSITIONING AXIS 4: PRICE-PERFORMANCE

This is a dimension of position that we all-too-often ignore. Yet, clarification is required here. When one speaks of price-related positioning, many people think in terms of the phrase 'value for money'. I believe that *every* piece of every brand sold must be offering 'value for money'; why else would anyone buy it?! To the buyer of a Mercedes sports car, it represents value for his money; just as the biscuit packet represents value for her money to the buyer of a pack of ordinary glucose biscuits.

What many people really mean when they use the term 'value for money' is low priced brands. Yet that, as we just saw, is an incomplete application of the concept. Actually a more meaningful concept is that of 'price-performance.' Now, in general, the *performance* (or quality or reliability etc.) is directly related to the price. As Lalitaji said in the Surf commercials of the 80s, *'sasti cheez aur achhi cheez mein farq hota hai.'* (Translation: There is a difference between a *cheap item* and a *good quality item*). This relationship can be simply expressed in a graphic form. Figure 8.5 shows some illustrative examples pertaining to the car market.

Figure 8.5: Price-Performance of car models available in India

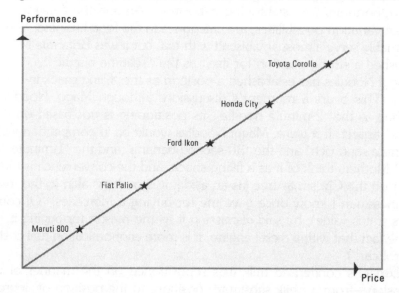

Figure 8.5 is, of course, conceptual and price-performance is clearly not a perfectly linear relationship. Nonetheless, this figure illustrates the principle. And the principle provides an opportunity to examine how brands occupy different positions or 'points' on the price-performance chart.

There are a couple of important points and watch-outs to note in this area.

One, too many brands in their communication, suggest that the brand offers 'great performance at low prices'. Just think of all the advertising you have seen with claims such as *'kam daam, badhiya kaam'* (Translation: Lower price, Great performance) or *'daam mein kam, kaam mein dam'* (Translation: Lower in price, power in the performance). The ultimate expression of this Utopian dream is a shop opposite Regal Cinema, in Mumbai, called 'Cheap & Best'! Yet there is a fundamental contradiction in such a proposition; and beyond a legitimate stretching of the imagination, it becomes incredible.

Two, a mere statement of the price-performance is likely to be of limited effectiveness. It works best, if there is an additional *meaning* provided (see Figure 8.6).

Figure 8.6: TV commercial: Peter England shirts and trousers

A well-dressed young man is sitting alone in the same restaurant...

She goes across and introduces herself. Then asks if he is, "Ravi?"

A woman is talking into her mobile phone to her mother about the prospective groom whom she is to meet in the restaurant.

The young woman continues into the phone, "I think I have spotted him!"

(*Contd.*)

She asks him how he finds India, after having lived abroad.

Just then the 'real' Ravi arrives, only to find that he has lost his girl to the Peter England man. VO: Peter England. Honestly impressive.

The man appears confused.

Shots of the man in different shirts and trousers. VO: Peter England shirts and trousers. By international designers. In international styles.

Figure 8.6 (Contd.)

And three, the price-performance positioning concept is just as valid at the high-price end as it is at the low-priced end.

As for the power of price-performance as a positioning approach, you need to look no further than the world's biggest corporation, Wal-Mart, whose strategy is single-mindedly focused on delivering superior price-performance. So much so that as a matter of policy, according to an article in *Fortune*, its managers are authorised to lower prices according to their own judgement, but are not allowed to increase the same without permission.

Consider some examples closer home. One of the most successful garment brands launched in the 90s was Peter England. It used its lower price-point— as compared to Louis Phillipe, Van Heusen, Arrow, etc.—to position itself at a new price-performance point, with the tagline 'the honest shirt', so as to add *meaning* (honesty) to the notion of low price (Figure 8.6). To have merely said 'From Rs.399' would have resulted in it being seen as just a cheaper shirt.

Another interesting example is the price-performance positioning of the Sonata brand of watches from Titan industries. Its range is advertised by the reassurance provided by the 'Tata' name, *not* the Titan name. It therefore allows Titan Industries to offer a lower-priced range to prospects, without the potentially negative effect of associating a cheap range, with the otherwise premium Titan brand.

Yet another example, this time involving a high-priced item, is the Octavia from Skoda. Here, the brand very clearly flags a high price-performance positioning.

Other examples of price-performance positioning involve offering higher-order performance at the same/similar price, as shown in Figure 8.7.

This often takes the form of a *supplementary benefit* that improves perceived performance. Examples would include the kind of extras offered by hotels, such as 'free stay in parents' room for 2 children below 12' or 'complementary airport transfers' or 'free use of health clubs.'

Similar 'extra-performance' may be cued by an additional servicing/check by a car battery brand, or a longer-period warranty by a ceiling fan manufacturer.

POSITIONING AXIS 5: BENEFIT OR FUNCTIONALITY

This is, of course, the 'mother' of all positioning dimensions; the one most commonly used. It is based on the basic premise that consumers don't buy products, they buy benefits or functionality. Looking at the major leading brands in most categories helps us understand this dimension.

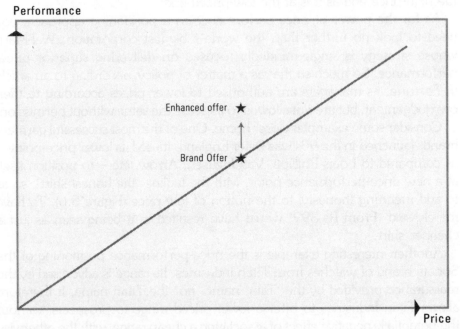

Figure 8.7: Creating an enhanced Price-Performance offer

Think of the benefits offered by these brands:

Detergents:
Wheel
Tide

Coffee:
Nescafe
Bru

Car Batteries:
Amaron
Exide

SUVs:
Sumo
Scorpio

Paints:
Tractor emulsion
Berger Weathercoat

Positioning by benefit or functionality is so common that it is often—mistakenly—assumed to be the only approach. As we saw earlier, several other approaches are possible.

As an exercise, fill the Positioning Grid shown as the Action Point for this chapter for your brand, and its main competitors.

POSITIONING VS EXECUTION

In thinking about positioning, it is important to remember that there is the danger of confusing *executional differences* with *differentiated* positions.

Try this exercise with the pairs of competing brands shown below: Study the advertising for each, consider their advertising tag lines, and think of what benefit position each brand occupies.

Optical whiteners:
Ujala
Robin Blue

Hair oil:
Dabur Amla Hair Oil
Bajaj Sevashram Bramhi Amla Hair Oil

Cars:
Ford Ikon
Accent Viva

Hair colour:
Garnier Nutrisse
L'Oreal Excellence

Not easy to see the differences in positioning between closely competing brands, is it? Many of you, if your brand operates in highly competitive categories, might have felt that positioning seems to be an inadequate concept to build differentiated brand perceptions. All the leading brands seem to be saying—more or less—the same thing in terms of the benefits offered, the price-performance delivery, and the time and place of use.

And in coping with this reality, brands move away from the very essence of positioning: That a brand must stand for a simple, memorable association or 'position'. The brands then attempt to 'add dimensions' to the position. Consider what Garnier is attempting with the Fortifying shampoo advertised here. Is this positioned against Clinic All Clear as an anti-dandruff shampoo? Where does it stack up against Head & Shoulders?

As the competition in more and more categories increases, there is a need to go beyond positioning. But looking at the Positioning Grid in your category is a useful stage of analysis, before we move to the concepts discussed in the next chapter.

Figure 8.8: Press advertisement: Garnier shampoo

We began this chapter by going back to the basics of positioning. We saw how Al Ries puts it: Positioning is not what you do to the product; it's what you do to the mind of the prospect. It's how you differentiate the brand in the mind…Positioning focuses on the perceptions of the prospect not the reality of the brand.

We also saw that there are two 'ends' to the positioning effort; the intention of the marketer and the result achieved. The actual position a brand achieves or occupies, is not the one intended by the marketer, but the perception that finally exists in the mind of the consumer.

In this context, it is important to remember that the reality of the brand places limits on what can be achieved. So, although the focus of positioning is perceptions and not the reality of the brand, the perceptions of the prospect cannot be entirely dissociated from the reality.

Positioning is a concept most useful in competitive markets and helps you to build strong bonds with a specific set of consumers, that is, the segment, you have decided to address, even if that means giving up other consumers. Indeed, you must not forget that powerful positioning is as much about deciding what to forgo, as it is about choosing the area to focus your efforts.

We saw that the different dimensions on which brands can be positioned are:

Positioning Axis 1: Product Category: We saw that the strategy of positioning a brand with reference to an entire product category works in two kinds of scenarios. The first is when a product innovation is involved.

The second scenario when one can position a brand against a category, is when a brand can serve a particular need being served by a single large brand, or a generic product.

Positioning Axis 2: Target Group: This can be a strong axis for positioning if there are no other brands serving a particular niche target group. For this reason, the target group based approach works better in cases where the target is defined in other than merely demographic terms.

Positioning Axis 3: Usage Patterns: We saw that in many categories there are limited variations in time or manner of usage. Nonetheless, we saw examples of brands like Britannia Marie and Milkmaid condensed milk, which have established strong positions along the usage dimension.

Positioning Axis 4: Price—Performance: This is a dimension of position that is often ignored or misunderstood. We saw that many people think only of low priced brands when they think of positioning brands on this axis. However, we noted that a more meaningful concept, is that of 'price-performance.'

Positioning Axis 5: Benefit Or Functionality: This is the most commonly used of all positioning dimensions and is based on the basic premise that consumers don't buy products, they buy benefits or functionality.

Finally, we saw that in highly competitive categories, positioning sometimes seems to be an inadequate concept to build differentiated brand perceptions, with all the leading brands saying more or less the same thing.

In the next chapter we look at some ways of thinking about brands that go beyond positioning.

Chapter 8: Action Point
Positioning: Positioning Grid

	Your brand	Competitor A	Competitor B	Competitor C
Brand name				
Positioning axis:				
1. Product category/ Specific competitor				
2. Target group				
3. Usage patterns				
4. Price-performance				
5. Benefit/functionality				

Beyond Positioning

More on Identifying what can make your Brand Unique

Overview

At one time, in Hindi films you had two main male characters and two main female characters. You had the hero and the villain, and the heroine and the vamp.

You needed the vamp to wear the bikinis and do the cabaret dance songs, because the heroine had to be virginal. The vamp smoked, drank, slept with the villain—she was the antithesis of the heroine. But when the heroines started wearing revealing clothes, and dancing in cabaret songs, there was no need for the vamp anymore.

Once the heroine had been modernized there was no place for the vamp. She had been made redundant by the repositioning of the heroine.

In the previous chapter we noted that if your brand operates in a highly competitive category, you might have felt that positioning had limitations as a concept to build differentiated brand perceptions. All the leading brands seem to be saying more or less the same thing in terms of the benefits offered, the price-performance delivery and the time and place of use.

In this chapter, we will look at some of the other approaches we can use to differentiate brands.

We will look specifically at two approaches: Emotional bonds and Archetypes, and how they can be used to develop Power advertising.

THE LIMITATIONS OF POSITIONING

In the previous chapter we saw how Positioning as a concept can suggest ways that a brand can use to establish a *relevant difference*, in the prospect's mind, with respect to competing brands.

However, there are several situations where it is worth looking at concepts beyond positioning to see how you can differentiate a brand. Here are some reasons why it may be necessary to do so.

1. POSITIONING INELASTICITY

In today's context of the extremely high cost of launching new brands, brand extensions are an important string to the marketer's bow. Yet, while you may extend the *brand name,* you need to consider whether the *position* can also be extended.

Let us consider Pears Soap in today's context. The original amber coloured soap, which consumers saw as a glycerine soap, was positioned as the soap that keeps skin looking young (one of the earliest baselines used in Pears advertising was, 'Some complexions just never grow up'). The very definition of a promise of *keeping* skin young, suggests that the appeal would be to a slightly older woman, perhaps in her early thirties, who is beginning to worry about 'aging' skin.

Now, however, there is a green, Oil-Free Pears soap, which promises an anti-pimple benefit. Is the original position valid for this variant that clearly targets much younger consumers? Can it be extended to embrace the new benefit?

There is a third Pears variant that offers the protection of mint against germs. Is the original position valid for this one? Can the original promise be extended to embrace the second, new benefit?

Of course, one can think of the Pears position as have been 'extended' to become 'the skin-care soap' which encompasses all these variants. Yet, by the very act of being *general* enough to include them all, the specificity, which is the strength of the idea of positioning, is weakened.

Consider another brand, Vicks, which has even more brand extensions; and, moreover, across different product categories. Here are some products that bear the Vicks name:

Vicks Vaporub
Vicks Cough Syrup
Vicks Cough Drops
Vicks Pain Balm
Vicks Formula 44

What is the position occupied by each? And, by the mother brand?

As brands find it preferable to extend an existing brand, rather than launch a new one in many situations, more marketers are going to find the concept of positioning being stretched thin.

2. PRODUCT AND POSITIONING

A second limitation of the notion of positioning is that it often rests on a product difference that consumers recognize. The original Liril 'freshness' position was intimately linked to the fact that it was a lime soap. Lifebuoy's 'protection against germs' position rests on its anti-bacterial ingredients. Godrej Pentacool refrigerators are positioned as the 'fastest cooling' refrigerators based on their five-side cooling design.

What happens when such product differences disappear with the growth in competition? Liril's freshness position, with lime at the heart of its claim, became less meaningful when Nima, Cinthol and other soaps also offered variants with lime.

Similarly, the notion of a particular position such as 'germ protection' may get vitiated as several contenders; Lifebuoy, Dettol and Pears (with mint) attempt to position themselves as 'germ protection' soaps.

Take yet another product category. Think about how much difference in positioning have Real, Tropicana, and other fruit drinks achieved; given that they all come in Tetrapak packaging, and are all 'real' fruit juices with no preservatives added (see Figure 9.1).

When it comes to edible oils, sunflower oil is sunflower oil is sunflower oil. Most brands of sunflower oil even import the sunflower oil from the same country. In packaged rice again, by definition, all brands of Basmati rice share the product commonality of being Basmati rice. In bottled water, what you get is water in a bottle!

This is not to say that positioning is impossible without product differences, or different benefit offers. Rather, it is to point out that without these, very important *axes for positioning* are no longer available.

3. 'Forced' Positions

As competition grows, some brands attempt to create 'forced' or 'artificial' positioning differences. These are differences, which might appear meaningful on paper, but are of no significance to the prospects' point of view and bear no relation to meaningful differentiation.

As an example, think of the launch of the 'Talking' washing machine some time ago. Now you may have the only 'Talking washing machine' position, but is it likely to be meaningful? And what next—a toaster with a sense of humour?!

4. The 'Changing Goalpost' Problem

Another limitation of positioning is what happens when categories evolve. Features, functionalities and benefits which were at one point differentiators for a brand and permitted positioning, can become meaningless as *all* the brands in a category begin to offer the same characteristics.

Figure 9.1: TV commercial: Real fruit juice

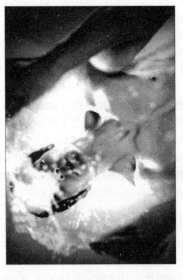

A man returns home after work. He approaches the bathroom to freshen up.

Cut to the shot where he splashes orange juice on his face.

MVO: "There's nothing like the refreshing goodness of real fruits. There's nothing like...

...Real Activ." Closing shot of the freshened up man. MVO and Super: 'Real Activ, Get Fresh, Get Activ.'

Hero Honda held the 'fuel-efficient bike' position when it was the first 4-stroke bike and promised 85 km per litre in its launch campaign, 'Fill it, shut it, forget it.' Can it hold on to that position now, when there are a host of motorcycles offering fuel economy around 80 km per litre; some even promising over 100 km per litre? So, does Hero Honda still occupy the fuel-efficient bike position?

In a much shorter time-band, features such as voice mail, ring tone options, SMS, MMS, built-in cameras, WAP and so on, have become standard features of mobile phone handsets and services. So how do you see the positions that Airtel, Hutch (Orange) and BPL Mobile occupy?

There is also another dimension to the changing reference frame, as technological progress blurs the boundaries of categories. Until a couple of years ago, Kodak cameras competed with other cameras. Today they compete with Nokia and Samsung mobile phones equipped with cameras.

In a somewhat similar way, the Sony Walkman competed with the personal stereos made by other consumer electronics brands. Today it competes with a computer manufacturer, Apple and the iPod.

Think of all the brands that have declined, or are on the verge of extinction, as the competitive landscape had changed.

5. POSITIONING MIRAGES

The fifth limitation of positioning is that, in the absence of clear *dimensions* of form and function, the concept itself becomes ephemeral in several categories. In detergents, one might think of being 'gentle on clothes' or 'cleaning power'—and so on—as different dimensions on which one can position brands.

Yet, how many dimensions can you think of on which you could consider positioning different brands of perfume? What about brands of Scotch whiskey?

Another development, which has taken place over the recent past, is the extent to which brands have become the language of self-expression—the words and the phrases that describe us. A line from one of the earliest campaigns for Vimal sarees and dress material stated this thought evocatively and explicitly: 'A woman expresses herself in many languages. Vimal is one of them'.

Rolls Royce, Patek Phillipe and Hermes have always been personal statements and expressions of taste and class, but a new level of 'I am the brands I use' has been reached when people are willing to become mobile posters for Adidas, Tommy Hilfiger and Nike, who often put the brand name as the key design element on their garments!

In this context, 'positioning' the brand with reference to the competition is not enough: The brand must be seen by the prospect in relation to what he/she think or want to believe about themselves.

BEYOND POSITIONING

When you are developing advertising in situations like the ones discussed in the previous section, we must look beyond positioning.

Although Reis & Trout said the Positioning Era replaced the Image Era, terms such as Brand image and Brand personality are alive and kicking. Think of the fairly typical Brand Image studies many marketers use. These cover a host of associations that brands have and include their attributes, performance characteristics, benefits, as well as its 'personality' characteristics. This is why, for instance, the dimensions covered in a Brand Image study on detergent powders might include all of the following:

- o Dissolves easily (attribute)
- o Generates lots of lather (performance characteristic)
- o Is gentle on delicate clothes (benefit)
- o Is chosen by modern housewives (personality dimension)

Brand personality, as one particular aspect of brand image, refers to a sub-set of these associations. Let us spend a little time understanding this concept. (Some companies use the term 'brand character' instead of brand personality. In principle, the idea is quite similar.)

As practitioners of advertising tried to understand the way consumers choose and grow loyal to brands, one of the concepts, which emerged, was that of likening a brand to a person. It is not unreasonable to think in these terms, given the predilection all of us have towards granting an anthropomorphic interpretation to things. Think, for instance, of the way we speak of how one's car was 'behaving temperamentally', or how we refer to the 'robustness' of a certain beer, or the 'masculinity' of a particular motorbike! It seems we just can't help thinking about things as possessing 'human' characteristics!

The notion, that we can attribute human-like characteristics to inanimate objects, has been applied to extend the traits used to describe humans, to also describe brands. So, terms such as 'warm', 'trustworthy', 'approachable', 'respected' and so on, are used to describe brands, and Brand personification emerges. It is a very useful notion, as long as you keep some things in mind.

Here are some of the limitations of the notion of brand personification, observed in practice in the Indian context:

CATEGORY IMPERATIVES

One, there are certain 'category imperatives' that limit the range of personality traits that a brand can—or would seek to-acquire.

A brand in the OTC (over the counter) medicine or healthcare or the baby products category almost certainly will have to display personality traits like 'warm', 'caring', and 'dependable.' You can see this in communication for brands from Johnson & Johnson to Aquaguard to Vicks Vaporub comparing the love and care it offers to a mother's love.

Brands in the financial services category will be under pressure to a 'reliable', 'trustworthy', 'knowledgeable' etc. personality.

Therefore while theoretically there may be a very wide range of personality traits in humans, the ones that have a good 'fit' with each product category would be fairly limited. And if *all* baby care products have warm, caring personalities, or most financial services brands are perceived as having trustworthy, knowledgeable personalities, how different will they appear to the person who has to choose between these brands?

Brands *can* break out of these 'category imperatives'—for instance, a bank may attempt to be seen as radically different in the way they work, and seek to display an 'iconoclastic' personality trait. However, such a strategy would run contrary to generally accepted consumer beliefs that banks should be stable, conservative (even if contemporary), prudent, and so on. And by and large, the returns on efforts aimed at changing strongly held beliefs are very low!

CONCEPT SOPHISTICATION

The idea of a brand having a personality like a human's, also has another limitation in terms of applicability: it is a concept which relatively less sophisticated (perhaps less educated) consumers do not understand very well. I have often found that it is not very easy for less educated or less sophisticated consumers to think in this way, and they are unable to think of or describe brands (of detergent cake or tea or whatever) as being different from each other in terms of being 'friendly' or 'modern' or 'helpful.' (A typical reaction you may hear is: 'What do you mean WYZ soap is friendly?!')

If the target group for your brand is of this type, the idea of brand personality must be used with some caution.

BRAND PERSONALITY VS ENDORSER PERSONALITY

One of the routes often used in an attempt to imbue a brand with a certain personality, is to use a celebrity endorser for the brand, whose personality will hopefully 'rub-off' on to the brand. (Even when celebrities are not used, the models used, the type of user portrayed, etc. imbue the brand with a 'personality' over time. Yet, since their own personalities are less well-defined than those of celebrities, their 'input-output' effect on brand personality may be assumed to be less 'overt'.

There are also some specific issues with using a celebrity endorser in India that you must consider. Firstly, we have a relatively small set of potential endorsers with mass appeal. And these are largely from the worlds of film and cricket.

Next, because of this limitation the same set of celebrities are used by a vast number of brands, and given *the variety and variation in these brands,* it is difficult to see what *specific personality traits the celebrity is contributing.* In the case of film stars, this problem is made even more complicated because in their films, they themselves *portray every possible personality trait!* So, which personality traits do consumers associate with a particular film star? For instance, which traits would you associate with Shah Rukh Khan?

- o Boyish, impulsive, fun-loving (as in *Kuchh Kuchh Hota Hai*)?
- o Intense, virtuous, conscientious (as in *Dilwale Dulhaniya Le Jaayenge*)?
- o Unpredictable, dark, obsessed (as in *Darr*)?
- o Romantic, vulnerable (as in *Devdas*)?
- o All of the above?

It is for this reason that it may be difficult to say what specific personality traits are being associated with the following brands, due to the celebrity endorser.

Table 9.1: Multiple brand celebrity endorsers

Brand	Celebrity endorser
Mayur suitings	Virendra Sehwag
Dabur toothpaste	Virendra Sehwag
Reliance Mobile	Virendra Sehwag
Reid & Taylor	Amitabh Bachchan
ICICI	Amitabh Bachchan
Nerolac Paints	Amitabh Bachchan
Dabur Chyavanprash	Amitabh Bachchan
Cadbury's	Amitabh Bachchan
MRF tyres	Sachin Tendulkar
Fiat Palio	Sachin Tendulkar
TVS Victor motorcycles	Sachin Tendulkar
Visa (cards)	Sachin Tendulkar

What do you think is the specific contribution of Sehwag to this TV commercial (Figure 9.2)? How different would it be if you used someone else—celebrity, or not?

Perhaps these celebrities remain larger than life—and larger than the brands they endorse!

What's the one thing that sums you up?

The final issue with brand personality is that it is made up of *several dimensions*. Let us consider the associations a brand of premium soap might have:

- o   Gentle
- o   Caring
- o   Feminine
- o   Luxurious
- o   Sensual
- o   Rich
- o   Soft
- o   Traditional

Now, what is the *key thing* that you would say about it? This is important because, as you increase the set of personality traits, the more overlap you are likely to find with other brands.

BRANDS & EMOTIONAL BONDS

Given the difficulties with positioning, and brand image that we have just considered, let us approach the issue of differentiation from another direction.

For a moment, think of the classmates you have/had in your school. Then, think of the associations that come to mind when you think of any one particular person, let's call him/her Person A. You may say that the associations, which come to mind, are:

Friendly
Contemporary
Fun-loving
Impulsive
Happy-go-lucky
…and so on.

Now, think of how many other classmates could be said to evoke the same associations. Undoubtedly, there will be others you can think of who may evoke similar associations.

Figure 9.2: TV commercial: Sehwag, for Reliance India Mobile

Turning towards his prospective son-in-law, the father says, "The pen is mightier than the bat"

Father-in-law-to-be is impressed, and calls for an early wedding

Father objects angrily about his daughter's choice of groom, "You have a PhD"

Sehwag (son-in-law) looks at his bat and begins to rattle off: "IMF conference in Washington, charity show by Clinton..."

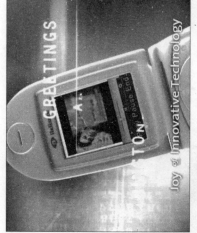

All laugh. VO: R World. News, videos, music, astrology, all at the press of a button

Sehwag says, cheekily, "You have your pen no, Sir?" VO: Reliance IndiaMobile. *Karlo duniya mutthi mein* (Translation: Catch the world in your hand.)

Sehwag refuses, "This is not an auspicious time, Sir"

The father-in-law-to-be wonders, "How is it I don't have all this on *my* phone?"

Figure 9.3: Press advertisement: Sachin Tendulkar, for Palio

Think, again, of two classmates who you consider close friends. Perhaps they, too, share many of these associations. Yet—and this is the key point being made—*what you share with each one of them is unique.*

- o   With one friend, what you share might be the *thrill and excitement* of high-adrenalin sports like skateboarding or BMX biking.
- o   With another, it might be the shared love of the *sentimentality* of Urdu poetry.

So, while these two friends might evoke many associations that are common, and are also common to several others, *the special relationship* you have with each of them is built around something that you share and which has an emotional resonance. *This is what Emotional Bonds are all about: shared emotional space.*

We know that a brand is far more differentiated when it focuses on *a single idea,* rather than when it attempts to acquire multiple associations. This, one might say, is Advertising 101: be single-minded.

Yes. It is; but with one important difference: The single notion referred to here, is not about the attributes or the benefits, or the personality of the brand, but about *a shared emotional space, the Emotional Bond.*

This concept of the single, intangible dimension represented in an abstract noun, has also been called 'Brand Essence'. That is a perfectly valid notion. But while the notion of Essence articulates *what the brand stands for* (beyond attributes, benefits, etc), we need something more, if we seek to establish a lasting relationship and commitment between the customer and the brand. Which is the reason why the term used is 'Emotional Bond'; it underlines the need to ensure that the intangible association must evoke an *emotional* response, and be seen as an overlap area between the prospect and the brand.

This is an important point to note. Because in the context of growing competition, the path to differentiation will be increasingly related to *intangibles.* In many ways one could say that branding begins where pure rationality ends (consider Figure 9.4)!

Figure 9.4: Competition and effective differentiation

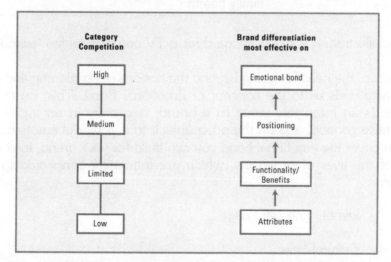

It is illuminating to understand what Figure 9.4 tells us. What it tells us is that, as competition increases, the *differentiators* are more likely to be based on intangible, emotional connections, rather than on attributes and functionality/performance-characteristics-related factors.

This is not to say that these are irrelevant; remember, we have discussed the multiple product-life-cycle phenomenon in Chapter 5. Indeed, even as you attempt to build an emotional bond for your brand, remember not to lose sight of the fact that there *must* be a functional underpinning to your brand. It is just that *differentiation* may not lie in that area. (Too many brands have focused only on the 'softer', intangible aspects, only to have customers wonder, after a period of time, whether there was any substance to the brand at all. The sizzle may be what gets the mouth to start watering, but *eventually* there better be a steak on the plate!)

Here are some examples of brands, which have established strong Emotional Bonds:

Brand	Emotional space shared
Axe	The (shared) thrill of *sexual fantasy* realized
KamaSutra	The (shared) *joy/ecstasy* of sex without inhibition or guilt
Dettol	The (shared) *concern* for daily family health
Pepsi	The (shared) *pleasure* of innocent mischief and pranks
Ferrari	The (shared) *excitement* of pushing the limits
Asian Paints	The (shared) *warm glow* of gathering around the family hearth

As an illustration is the storyboard for a TV commercial for Asian Paints (Figure 9.5).

To recap, the need for going beyond the notions of positioning and brand personality leads us to the concept of Emotional Bond. This, on the one hand adds an intangible value to a brand, necessary in an increasingly competitive context, and on the other links it to a powerful emotion.

To discover the emotional bond you can build for your brand, look at the areas of the lives of prospects, which are intimately connected to their emotions:

- o   Identity and self image
- o   Values
- o   Cultural links
- o   Attitudes

Let us consider some examples in each of these areas.

Figure 9.5: TV commercial: Asian Paints

A couple sprawls on the bed lazily as a sunbeam filtering through the window beckons a new day. *'kiska aasman hai'*

"Kamron mein kiski kalpana jhalakti hai? Is farsh par nange pair kiske bacche chalte hain?" A little boy jumps around his home in joy.

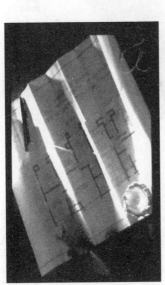

A blueprint unfurls on the table as the MVO states, *"Har ghar chup chaap se yeh kehta hai ki andar usmein kaun rehta hai"*

"Rang kehta hain kiska yeh jahaan hai." A young man hugs a shrivelling old lady as she interrupts her knitting to smile benignly at his gesture.

(Contd.)

Figure 9.5 (Contd.)

The woman strikes a proud pose against a wall, "*Kaun is makaan mein apna ghar basaata hai...*"

The couple shifts a heavy table to one corner of the room and plunks it down tiredly, as the MVO continues, '*ke andar usmein kaun rehta hai.*'

VO: "*Har ghar chup chaap se yeh kehta hai...*"

IDENTITY AND SELF IMAGE

In the deepest recesses of our heart, we hold an image of ourselves. It does not matter whether it is an image we aspire to attain, or a secret we hide, or a fantasy we cherish, or what we wish we were: all of these are just as 'real.'

This self-image is why a young man identifies with a Devdas: *he actually feels the pain* and pathos of the distressed lover in the film. Or why another walks with arms akimbo as he comes out of a martial arts film *a la* Bruce Lee: in his mind's eye, *he is Bruce Lee* in Enter the Dragon, going off to take on the evil Han. Or, for that matter, why a woman looks at a Tulsi in *Kyonki Saas Bhi Kabhi Bahu Thi*, and *sees a reflection of herself*—as taking care of the family, holding the family together against the assaults of a hostile world.

A Quantum Market Research study done in 2001, looked at some of the most popular TV soaps and presented the kind of images of women that were being portrayed. The popularity of the main protagonist in these soaps would suggest that large numbers of women in India find a reflection of their self-image in them. Here are some of the conclusions drawn (Figure 9.6) in the Quantum 'Woman of 2001' study, from an assessment of two popular TV serials of the time.

Raymond and the Complete Man: A long-running example of a brand that built an Emotional Bond based on an aspect of self-image is Raymond fabrics. 'The Complete Man' retained his sensitivity amidst the de-humanizing needs of a competitive world. He treated the woman in his life as an equal, he was a friend to a daughter; he paused to smell the flowers, even as he was successful in his profession. It was a self-image, especially empathetic to a large number of young, urban professionals coping with the new harsh realities of the business world in the 80s and 90s. The self-image allowed the young person to belong to the contemporary world of business and competition and yet retain 'eternal, human' values that set him apart from the totally mercenary persons around him. It created a bond with the shared 'belief in the larger eternal human values'.

Another powerful self-image—which also involves the reluctance to being part of the anonymous crowd—is the image which is reflected in everything that Apple Computers does. Whether it is the see-through, translucent look of the original iMac, the stylishness of the iPod, the creative potential of the iMovie and iPhoto software, or the innovativeness of the iMusic Store.

Indeed, not only the company's products but also its CEO, Steve Jobs, is the embodiment of the attitude of creative experimentation, which has built a strong bond around the shared space of 'creative iconoclasm', with its

Figure 9.6: Analyses of TV serials

Serial	Mythic Value	Myth Retold	Emerging Face of the Woman
Saans	• Savitri and Satyavan • Chaste wife • Loss of her husband • Her chaste virtue forces the gods to return her mate ↓ Power of chastity and commitment	• Priya is a good wife • Loses husband to another woman ↓ • She re-builds her life but remains chaste and virtuous ↓ • Her virtue forces the husband to return ↓ Power of virtue and perseverance	• Chaste • Committed • Ready to persevere • Self reliant • Completes the man • Femininity balanced

Kyonki Saas Bhi Kabhi Bahu Thi	• Myth of the mother goddess
	• Three dimensions of female power
	  - maya and delusion
	  - knowledge and wisdom
	  - creation and destruction
		• Extended family with:
		  - grandmother
		  - daughters-in-law
		  - grand daughter-in-law
		• Three facets of womanhood depicted
		• Grandmother represents knowledge and wisdom
		• Tulsi's mother-in-law represents maya + delusion
		• Tulsi represents the female principle of:
		  - creation
		  - destruction
		  - preservation
			• Multi-faceted persona
			• Good and bad co-exist and need to be balanced
			• Birth of the strategist

Courtesy: Quantum Market Research

customers. This bond that people from creative types in advertising, design and Hollywood, to school and college students share with Apple is so strong that they often think of themselves as 'Macolytes' and treat the annual MacWorld event like a pilgrimage!

As an exercise, think of the Emotional Bond your brand can build with consumers.

Figure 9.7: Press advertisement: From the 90s' Raymond campaign

Everyone should have a good friend like you.

Who helps steal mangoes from the neighbour's tree.

Who falls in love with the same girl.

Who beats you at chess.

Who can keep a secret.

Who can take your wrath.

And comfort you in sorrow.

A special person to learn from. To trust.

Someone who protects you.

Someone who never takes you for granted.

And grows closer to you with time.

Friend, buddy, the complete man.

Raymond

VALUES

Shared values are among the strongest bonds that exist between people; they also build strong bonds between brands and customers. Two of the values, which captured the imagination of people during the 70s and 80s, were the bases of bonds that two major international brands forged with their customers.

One of the dominant trends of thought in those post-Woodstock days was the sense of a 'world without borders', and the 'we are one world' ideals which took center-stage in music 'happenings' and in the growing sense that acts in one part of the world could affect all of us. The potential impact of global warming and uncontrolled exploitation in the remotest parts of the world became visible through the television screen-window in our homes, and created the backdrop for the Benetton brand's communication. The 'United Colours of Benetton' became a flag, if you will, for the belief that the world and its people were one. The Benetton logo was thus a badge and wearing a garment with it, was the equivalent of stating your allegiance to that flag, and the passport of a world-nation.

Another value, which was highlighted in approximately the same period and partially for common reasons, was the concern for the planet, and the importance of eco-friendly acts and practices. This environmental conscience was embodied by The Body Shop, and helped attract a large number of people who shared the value.

CULTURAL LINKS

Sometimes values are universal, as we saw in the examples of Benetton and The Body Shop. Others are magnified and made more 'real' when placed in a specific cultural context.

The Tata Salt campaign (Figure 9.8) launched in 2002–03, links the notion of brand honesty to the deeply-held Indian belief of being truthful and loyal to those 'whose salt one has eaten.' (It is summed up in the Hindi phrase *'aapka namak khaya hai'*). Here, the bond is built on the shared view that there is no greater honesty than that demonstrated by the one who has, in a manner of speaking, shared your salt.

However, one has to be watchful of changing cultural contexts that can make such efforts irrelevant.

In the 80's, Ruf-n-Tuf jeans linked the value of 'down-to-earth honesty' to an anti-western stance. The commercial for the brand which presented this perspective showed a blond westerner as a stereotypically arrogant youngster, who showed no respect for the older, 'rural' Indian, and acted in a superior manner—until the Ruf-n-Tuf wearer came to the aid of the villager and 'taught the upstart a lesson'.

All that may be very well; but this clearly became an irrelevant and meaningless viewpoint—as the economy opened up and more expatriates came to work in India, and the Indian consumers on their part adopted a host of international brands. It's a bit difficult to wear the 'son-of-the-soil' badge, while one wears a pair of Reeboks, slips on ones RayBans and sips a Pepsi! However, I think it was not the 'down-to-earth honesty' point of view, which had become redundant—it was the particular expression of it that became obsolete. With a different expression, the basic point of view could have remained meaningful.

The Action Point at the end of this chapter lists four areas of life to think about, in identifying the bases of Emotional bonds built around Identity and self image, Values, Cultural links and Attitudes.

ATTITUDES AND BELIEFS

Another powerful basis of building Emotional Bonds, is for a brand to reflect a particular attitude (by which I mean a *specific point of view*, rather than

Figure 9.8: TV commercial: Tata salt

... *farz apna tu nibha le pure ji jaan se*, plays in the background as the camera pans to a soldier.

...*jitna tu dega utna phir se mil jayega*... as a girl teaches an adult education class.

An opening shot of a man caressing a photograph... *de-de, de-de, khud ko de-de desh ke naam pe de*...

The next frame has a lady closing a tap... *katra, katra desh ke kam ayega*...

(Contd.)

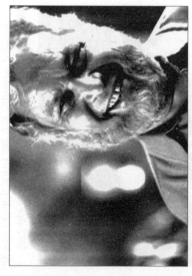

After that, an injured cricketer refusing a stretcher and playing on... *yaad rahe desh ka namak khaya hai.*

... as he too swears his loyalty to the nation, *"meine desh ka namak khaya hai".*

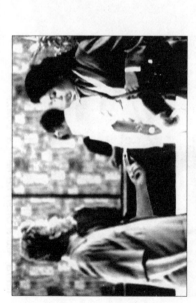

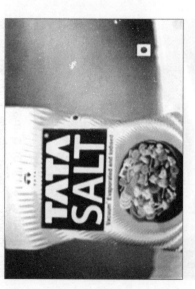

Next, a taxi driver declining a reward for returning a mobile phone left by the customer.

MVO: Tata *Namak, aisa khara namak, jiska kharapan desh ke caroron logo mein jhalakta hai...*

Figure 9.8 (Contd.)

the non-specific catchall manner in which the word 'attitude' is misused and abused!)

An attitude which appeals to a lot of young people today is that of the 'post-advertising man.' A person who is so cool, he has found *moksha* (liberation), beyond the 'overt' posturing of cool by lesser mortals who are still caught up in the *maya* (illusion) of consumerism! He is so cool that he doesn't need to be 'cool.' He is the Sprite drinker, who spurns *'gyan'* (philosophy, which is fancy in this case) for simple thirst quenching. The irony of course is that he would not be able to sustain this attitude, if in fact there was no advertising, which made the world aware of his imperviousness to advertising! But it is an interesting counter-point to the overt image-seeking conveyed by a host of youth-oriented brands.

ARCHETYPES

Another, very interesting approach to understanding the way brands can build lasting relationships with customers, is based on the Jungian notion of 'Archetypes'.

Jung defined archetypes as *'active, living dispositions that form and continually influence our thoughts, feelings and actions.'*

The 'archetype' is literally, an idealized, and even 'purified' form, a template of a kind of person, which seems to exist in the sub-conscious and is shared by men and women across societies. Their universality is the reason why they evoke strong emotional responses from deep down, and touch people with apparently diverse backgrounds—from the well-educated, well-to-do urbanite, to the uneducated, struggling, small-town dweller.

The archetypes are themes or templates that echo in stories in all cultures, because they reflect truths that are human and valid across time and space. These are the themes and templates that we encounter in myths and legends, in epics and nighttime children's stories, and in films and novels. They are themes that we relate and respond to, because they reflect the deepest aspects of what makes us human.

The application of this idea to brands has been developed exceptionally well by Margaret Mark and Carol S. Pearson in their seminal book, *The Hero and the Outlaw*. I would strongly urge readers to read it. In a nutshell, however, here is the set of 12 archetypes proposed by Mark and Pearson:

An important concept to understand is that the archetype is represented within people and is echoed in brands. Thus, for example, there is an 'Innocent' within a consumer, which relates to an 'Innocent' brand such as Pears soap.

1. ARCHETYPE: THE HERO

The Hero is a Crusader, a warrior, a fighter. He will fight against all odds, take on any challenge. He defends the weak, the helpless and helps them get what is rightfully theirs. Whenever there is oppression, there is a Hero who will rise.

Examples of the archetype in the world of books, films and entertainment: Amitabh Bachchan in *Zanjeer*, Aamir Khan in *Ghulam* and *Sarfarosh*, James Bond.

Examples of the archetype in brands: Red & White cigarettes, Bajaj Caliber (in the 'Unshakable' campaign), Nike.

2. ARCHETYPE: THE OUTLAW

The Outlaw is the Rebel, the Iconoclast, the revolutionary. He shocks and he offends those who are 'comfortable' with the way things are. He seeks to overturn the status quo...he operates outside the rules of the world. He is the outsider, the rallying point for those who want to overthrow the current state of things, and bring radical change.

Examples of the archetype in the world of books, films and entertainment: Amitabh Bachchan in *Deewar*, and *Trishul*, Shah Rukh Khan in *Baazigar*, Shammi Kapoor in *Junglee*, Eminem, Robin Hood.

Examples of the archetype in brands: Killer jeans, Virgin Airlines (also Virgin mobile, Virgin records, etc), Bacardi Blast

3. ARCHETYPE: THE MAGICIAN

The Magician is a creature who can make anything happen! She knows secrets hidden from the common man, and can make your dreams come true...can transform you.

Examples of the archetype in the world of books, films and entertainment: Prof. Higgins in *My Fair Lady*, Shah Rukh Khan in *Dil to pagal hai*, *The Lord of the Rings* and the Harry Potter series of books.

Examples of the archetype in brands: Bausch & Lomb contact lenses, Lux ('*Mujhme star jagaye*'), Kiwi all-purpose cleaner, Tide, Airtel 'Magic' Pre-paid cards.

4. ARCHETYPE: THE CREATOR

This is the Inventor, the artistic one, who finds self expression. The Creator makes imagination come to life.

Examples of the archetype in the world of books, films and entertainment: Howard Roark in *The Fountainhead* by Ayn Rand, Amadeus.

Examples of the archetype in brands: Apple Computers ('Think Different'), Lego, Asian Paints ('*Har ghar kuchh kehta hai*'), Sony Handycam.

5. ARCHETYPE: THE RULER

The Ruler is All-Powerful, and a leader of men and women. He is the writer of the laws and rules that define the world. He is the one you obey, the one who maintains order.

Examples of the archetype in the world of books, films and entertainment: Prithviraj Kapoor in *Mughal-e-Azam*, Don Corleone in *The Godfather*.

Examples of the archetype in brands: India Kings, Rolls Royce, IBM, Hugo Boss, Louis Vuitton

6. ARCHETYPE: THE REGULAR GUY

This is your 'guy next door', who is friendly, approachable, whom everyone knows as a nice guy. He fits in with all groups, because he is the nice guy who embodies all the good values of decency, honesty, empathy, and warmth.

Examples of the archetype in the world of books, films and entertainment: Shah Rukh Khan in *Kuchh Kuchh Hota Hai*, Kamal Hassan in *Saagar*, the characters in *Friends*, Rajesh Khanna in *Anand*, the protagonist in *It's a beautiful life*.

Examples of the archetype in brands: Santro ('The sunshine car'), Sprite.

7. ARCHETYPE: THE LOVER

This is the romantic, the one for whom you are the world! He brings sensuality, intimacy, love into your life. He makes you feel the most wonderful person in the world when you are with him. He makes you feel special, beautiful, desired.

Examples of the archetype in the world of books, films and entertainment: Humphrey Bogart in *Casablanca*, Casanova, Leonardo Di Caprio in *Titanic*, Rajesh Khanna in *Amar Prem*, Romeo or *Majnu*.

Examples of the archetype in brands: Nakshatra diamonds, Enamor undergarments, KamaSutra condoms, Maybelline, Palmolive Aroma range

8. ARCHETYPE: THE JESTER

He is the life of the party, the prankster, practical joker. Helps liven up things, there is never a dull moment when he is around. He makes you forget your worries, makes you laugh, and find fun and enjoyment.

Examples of the archetype in the world of books, films and entertainment: Aamir Khan in *Dil Chahta Hai*, Govinda in *Hero No.1*, Charlie Chaplin.

Examples of the archetype in brands: Alpenliebe Lollypop, Centre Shock chewing gum, Cadbury's Perk.

9. ARCHETYPE: THE CARE-GIVER

She is Florence Nightingale, full of gentleness, sympathy and caring. She is supportive, helpful, dependable in your hour of need. She nurtures and protects.

Examples of the archetype in the world of books, films and entertainment: *Mother India*.

Examples of the archetype in brands: Johnson & Johnson, Moov. Vicks Vaporub, ICICI Bank (*'Hum hain na'*), Saffola.

10. ARCHETYPE: THE EXPLORER

He is the one who refuses to be tied down, he is the one ready to move out at a moment's notice. He values his independence, seeks out new experiences and novelty. He is individualistic, non-conformist, the one who will be bored with the known and the commonplace.

Examples of the archetype in the world of books, films and entertainment: Indiana Jones, Capt. Picard in *Star Trek*, Jodie Foster in *Cosmos*.

Examples of the archetype in brands: Emirates Airlines. ('When was the last time you did something for the first time?'), Charms ('Charms is the spirit of freedom. Charms is the way you are'), Mitsubishi Pajero.

11. ARCHETYPE: THE SAGE

The man of the Mind. The seeker of knowledge. He is the one who will be analytical, will seek surety, and in turn is the one that others turn to for guidance, advise, expertise.

Examples of the archetype in the films and entertainment world: The Jedi in *Star Wars*, Morpheus in *The Matrix*.

Examples of the archetype in brands: NIIT, Franklin Templeton.

12. ARCHETYPE: THE INNOCENT

The child: uncorrupted, pure, optimistic, trusting, happy.

Like a child—simple, a dreamer, full of goodness, without guile and cunning.

Examples of the archetype in the world of books, films and entertainment: Hrithik Roshan in *Koi Mil Gaya*, Jaya Bhaduri in *Guddi*.

Examples of the archetype in brands: Pears Soap, Johnson & Johnson Baby shampoo, Britannia Treat biscuits.

Think of the most powerful brands you know. Do they represent or embody an archetype? Does *your brand* express an archetype: A universal, compelling set of qualities that typify a kind of person who evokes an emotional response—because they represent a basic aspect of ourselves as human beings?

Summing Up

In closing, one would say that there are situations when the notion of positioning is inadequate and one must look at ways that go further, such as Emotional Bonds or Social archetypes, to build brand preferences. Of course it is possible for die-hard votaries of positioning to say that even advertising based on say, using the Hero archetype, is just a way of 'positioning the brand as a Hero'. That seems to me to be stretching the point, and fails to recognize that there are other ways of approaching the problem at hand. The question is not one of defending positioning against all criticism but of realizing that there are other principles, which are worth thinking about, in creating brand differentiation, preference and Power advertising.

We have seen that there are at least two other powerful ways of thinking about brand differentiation: Emotional bonds and Archetypes.

We saw that the Emotional Bond is about a shared emotional space, that goes beyond the attributes or the benefits, or the personality of the brand.

And we saw that the emotional bond for a brand is linked to the areas in the lives of prospects, which are intimately connected to their emotions:

- *Identity and self image*
- *Values*
- *Cultural links*
- *Attitudes*

On the other hand, the 'archetype' is literally, an idealized template of a kind of person, which seems to exist in the sub-conscious and is shared by men and women across societies.

Their universality is the reason why they evoke strong emotional responses from deep down, and touch people with apparently diverse backgrounds.

The archetypes are themes that echo in stories in all cultures, because they reflect truths that are human and valid across time and space. These are the themes we relate to and respond to, because they reflect the deepest aspects of what makes us human.

An important concept we saw is that the archetype is represented within people and is echoed in brands. Thus for example, there is an 'Innocent' within a consumer, which relates to an 'Innocent' brand such as Pears soap.

Chapter 9: Action Point
Checklist for Developing Emotional Bonds

These are not exhaustive lists. They are intended to serve as thought-starters to think about how you can develop Emotional Bonds

Building Emotional Bonds related to Identity & Self image
LIFE CONTEXT: Look into the mind, heart and soul of your target group and their lives.
Pastime/activities
Feelings
Fears, concerns
Dreams, desires
Language
Ambitions

Building Emotional Bonds related to Values
VALUES: What values does the target group relate to?
Honesty vs dishonesty
Hardworking vs happy go lucky
Conventional vs unconventional
Individualistic vs conformist
Frugal vs spendthrift
Idealist vs practical
Respectful vs irreverent
EMOTIONAL HOOKS: Think of the emotions, concerns and fears your target group face.
Achievement
Freedom
Altruism
Self indulgence
Pride/humility

Building Emotional Bonds related to Cultural Links
RELATIONSHIPS: What are the most and least important relationships in their lives? Why?
Parents
Siblings
Friends
Women/girl (Man/boy) friends
Colleagues
Superiors at work
Neighbourhood peers
EMOTIONAL HOOKS: Think of the emotions, concerns and fears your target group face.
Inspiration
Escapism
Charity
Faith
Nationalism

Building Emotional Bonds related to Attitudes
ATTITUDES: What feelings and attitudes do the target group relate to?
Optimistic vs pessimistic
Aggressive vs submissive
Indulgent vs not indulgent
Clever vs. ordinary
Has an opinion vs does not have an opinion
Risk taker vs risk averse
Fun loving vs serious
Friendly vs unfriendly/aloof
Sophisticated vs unsophisticated
Leader vs follower
Seeking excitement in life vs equanimity in life

Active vs passive
Creative vs not creative
Romantic vs unromantic
Unique vs commonplace
Forceful vs quiet
Expressive vs repressed
EMOTIONAL HOOKS: Think of the emotions, concerns and fears your target group face.
Stress relief
Escapism
Success
Status
Style
Romance/Love
Camaraderie
Pure pleasure
Confidence
Power
Respect

Chapter 9: Action Point
Checklist for Archetypes

Archetype	Characteristics which suggest Brand fit
The Hero	
The Outlaw	
The Magician	
The Creator	
The Ruler	
The Regular guy	
The Lover	
The Jester	
The Care-giver	
The Explorer	
The Sage	
The Innocent	

The Brief: The Creative Springboard

Pulling all the Threads Together

Overview

There is an old joke: Every man wants a wife who is beautiful, understanding, economical, and a good cook. But you can't have them all—the law allows only one wife.

Single mindedness is just as important in the matter of an advertising brief.

All the preceding analysis, all the thinking applied to understand the market context, the competition, the consumer, and so on, has but one critical objective: the development of a creative brief which will inspire the actual creative product. Whether it is a press advertisement, or a television commercial, or a hoarding design, or a piece of Direct Mail or whatever.

Too often, the task of preparing a creative brief is seen as an exercise of 'summarisation' of all the analytical effort and output. Of 'compressing' all that into the briefing format which the organization uses. Unfortunately.

'Unfortunately', because there is no 'magic' in compression. Have you ever seen a compression machine compress scrap metal into cubes? That is all that mere compression or summarization will achieve. It will reduce the volume of space occupied but it will still remain what it was to start with.

Instead, think of the task of preparing the creative brief as an act of 'distillation.' Of sifting through the analysis done, to isolate those stimuli that will lead to breakthrough, powerful communication. The act of doing this is as creative an act, as that of writing the script for the final television commercial or creating the final press advertisement. The only difference is that a Creative Brief is a piece of work which is aimed only at the creative team, while the final television commercial is aimed at the thousands of prospects for your product or service.

At one level, *all* Creative Briefs come down to a single set of points. And the formats and systems used by different agencies differ more in letter than in spirit. All of them, essentially, seek answers to the following questions:

- What is the objective/purpose of the advertising
- Who is the intended target of the advertising
- What do we have to 'offer' to the target
- Why will the target find our offer interesting
- What are the insights we have about this target which will allow us to create compelling communication
- What is the 'personality' (or archetype) we want our brand to have
- Are there any specific do's and don'ts that need to be followed (these may be a matter of legal/statutory requirement or marketing guidelines for the brand)

Creative Briefs are written day in and day out, and most of them are treated exactly the way an Art Director I know, once did. He pointed to the waste paper basket, and told the executive who had brought the brief, to, 'put it in the In-Tray.'

Before you say that this behaviour seems typical of the behaviour of arrogant creative types, ask yourselves this: Would you 'buy' anything if it did not interest, stimulate, motivate, or excite you? Well, why do you think the creative team is any different?! So, how do you write a brief that will excite and stimulate them? Let us go back and review the key issues and action points from earlier chapters.

1. MARKETS IN FLUX

We noted that as market dynamics change, many of the characteristics that define the 'contours' of a market are themselves in a state of change. Viewed in one way, this may appear to be creating a condition where planning is difficult because the *context,* created by specific characteristics is itself changing. Here are some of the features of a market, which might be changing.

- Price *categories merging into a 'spectrum of price points'*: When there are clear 'gaps' in the prices of different clusters of brands, it is possible to define these as separate price-bands. However, as competition increases, often, the gaps get filled up with offerings priced at intermediate points. This makes it difficult to define a clear set of competitors based on price, because even a relatively small move up or down in price, offers new alternatives to a customer.

○   *The erosion of clear category divisions:* In many cases marketers have learnt that customers will not 'stay within' the category definitions the industry uses. To begin with, these categories are often used as convenient shorthand within the industry; but, over time, they come to assume a sense of concreteness that is not representative of the consumer reality! For example, the categorization of two wheelers into scooters and motorcycles became less relevant as the fuel economy characteristic of motorcycles changed with the launch of the 4-stroke bikes. In other products too, this category-diffusion has taken place. Think of the difference between colourful 'casual shirts' and white or pastel coloured 'office shirts' which disappeared, as Friday dressing became acceptable across the week. The same is true of shampoos in some ways—from a stage where there were shampoos and others were shampoos with conditioners, today most shampoos have conditioners; and another differentiator has become a category basic.

○   Finally, the bases of competitiveness may themselves be undergoing change. Whether it is product, technology, distribution or any other characteristic. For example, think of the branch network, essentially an aspect of distribution, which was a major strength of the older Indian banks. This feature became less relevant as the introduction of ATMs, Phone Banking and so on, made 'physical distribution' less relevant and paved the way for the rapid growth of newer, private Indian banks as well as foreign banks who had smaller branch networks than those of Public sector banks.

We saw that with such rapid developments taking place in market after market, it is important to conduct an Assessment of Market Changes. Think of the changes taking place in the market you are addressing: Make this Point Number 1 in your brief.

Are younger girls becoming more make-up conscious? Is the considered set of 'basic grooming aids' expanding? Is the resistance to the use of certain products by parents reducing? Does lipstick seem to be moving from being 'makeup' to part of 'daily grooming'? Social changes such as these could suggest a change in the basic market with far-reaching possibilities, if you are in the grooming or cosmetics business.

Take another category. Look at how the cellular phone has evolved from just a mobile phone, to a lifestyle accessory. Do they need to make a fashion statement? Are features, such as Bluetooth, considered essential features? Is the mobile phone also the 'portable music' system of users? Is it a 'portable' entertainment console'? Is a camera in the phone considered a basic feature? As a pointer, remember that in 2004, for the first time, more cellular phones with cameras were sold, than actual stand-alone digital cameras!

Figure 10.1: Extending the benefit-space of mobile phones

And it is not just cell phone manufacturers who are responding to these changes.

Here is an example of how a cellular service provider is offering a 'feature', which has nothing to do with making or receiving calls.

Figure 10.2: Press advertisement: Hutch, offering games with the cellular service

Look at banking services. Do customers consider a wide ATM network essential? What about a Debit card? How much of a differentiator is Phone banking? Do the customers seem to want their bank to be their *financial service center,* rather than just a place where they have a savings account? How important are lockers? (Not too long ago these were important determinants of preference for a bank)

These are early opportunity signals that can help your brand take a leading-edge stance in the market. Excite the creative team by creating a living, evocative picture of the new reality. As an example, it was the emerging reality of younger girls adopting the usage of make up, along with the insight that this also represented their growing independence, that set the context for the Elle 18 communication a few years ago.

2. THE MARKETING DRIVERS AND THE SOURCE OF BUSINESS

Within the view you have formed of the emerging marketplace, you will need to make judgments about two key factors.

    (a) *The key driver of your brand:* Here you will have to consider which aspect—the user group, the product/service, the price or the distribution, you can leverage to competitive advantage.

Remember, these are not characteristics, which are 'other than the communication', but can be the very underpinning of the communication strategy and plan.

(b) *The source of business:* This is based on your judgment of whether you expect your users/buyers to be the old user or the new user of the category. And whether you expect your users/buyers to be using it in terms of the old usage patterns or do you see new usage patterns from which you expect to gain business.

The foregoing may appear extraneous to the communication decision, but it is a step that can help you identify a focus for your communication you might miss otherwise.

For example, consider a brand of TV, which has a significant distribution network in rural areas (or is planning such an expansion). This situation opens up the possibility of leveraging distribution by focusing on upgrading current TV set owners. The brand can create schemes and programmes to incentivise current TV owners in urban areas, to move up to newer sets, and recondition the old sets, which can be sold at affordable prices in the hinterland.

Or, take the way in which *Maharashtra Times*, a major Marathi newspaper tackled the 'new users' represented by youngsters. *Maharashtra Times* used an interesting tactic in early 2004 to address these new users. Young persons, even in homes where the older generation read the Marathi paper, were less likely to read it. The communication effort addressed this younger group, by showing how *Maharashtra Times* could actually be an aid to the young person in achieving her new-age ambitions; in the particular case shown in the commercial the young girl's dream of becoming a fashion designer.

The commercial shows how a young girl who wants to be a fashion designer finds information in the *Maharashtra Times*, which helps her in learning more about fashion and design.

Step 2 in developing the brief then, is to decide what can actually drive your business and where the business opportunity lies. This judgment could well give the brand a head start and help it establish a differentiated identity, by catching a social trend at the rise of the wave of change.

3. SEGMENTATION AND TARGETING

This involves choosing the specific set of prospects you will focus on. This is the area where briefs are often the weakest. Here are the watch-outs, which will help you avoid some common pitfalls.

(i) A description that includes *every possible user* of the product or service is clearly not identifying a *segment,* which—by definition—must be a *special subset* of the total users. Therefore, for example, if you are selling a hair-dryer, then 'people with hair' is not a segment, it is your entire potential universe of users! Now, however, if you define your segment as 'people with *curly* hair', you have an interesting possible segment to focus on. Understanding the needs, motivations, concerns, fears and so on of the subset of people who have curly hair will enable you to define and target a meaningful segment.

(ii) However, understanding the needs, motivations, and so on is not enough. The second critical thing to remember, is that your definition of the segment must create an *internally homogenous* group (i.e. it must define a group of people whose members are similar in one or more significant ways); but just as importantly, it must also create a group which is *externally heterogeneous* (i.e. the members of the group are dissimilar to those outside the group, or different from the groups being targeted by your competition, in one or more significant ways). This is an aspect that is often overlooked.

Let us take an example. Suppose someone has defined the segment for a brand of readymade shirts as, 'young, successful, westernized, urban males'. This is certainly an *internally homogenous* group, but is it *externally heterogeneous?*

No, because this is no different from the group that would be the target of practically *every* brand of readymade shirt. On the other hand, if you just changed the last word in the above segment definition to 'females', you may be addressing a genuinely distinct segment: 'young, successful, westernized, urban females'.

There is some interesting work in addressing new, uncommon segments, which is to be seen in the communication for diamond jewellery brands. The generic communication for diamond jewellery has for years addressed the typical boy-wants-to-marry-girl target, and presented diamonds as a reflection of his love. Its variation of man-who-wants-to-celebrate-a-wedding-anniversary is a mere time-shifted picture of the same person. However, the Asmi brand of diamond jewellery speaks to a different segment. It addresses women who see diamonds as a *reflection of themselves,* and their sense of self-worth. Asmi diamonds are not bought by a man as an expression of love for a woman; they are bought by the woman for herself, as a statement of her individuality.

Of course it is not necessary that you *must* use segmentation as the most important axis for differentiation; you may well choose to follow a non-segmented approach and use some other basis for building distinctiveness

Figure 10.3: Press advertisement: Asmi Diamonds

for your brand—such as the usage of your brand, as done by Milkmaid—but do so after due consideration, not as a matter of mechanically filling up a section in your creative brief. (Avoid being like the man who tick-marked 'yes' in the column under 'Sex' on his passport application!)

(iii) *The group vs the individual:* This is crucial. The segment as a group of persons is important for assessing the size of the market, or for media planning decisions. But the actual communication is received by—and thus must address—individuals. This individual is the one that your creative brief must describe. The Creative brief must speak of the *target person*, not the target group.

One more caution: Do *not* describe a person who is the 'average' of all the people that you are targeting, with 'average' values of age, education opinions or whatever. 'Average' people are boring; and advertising that speaks to boring people will be boring. Therefore, it is important that in the Creative brief, the target being described be an individual. For instance, 'young, attractive, fun-loving, outgoing' describes pretty much every young film actress. But if you were to add 'with a barely concealed air of mischief', Kajol or Preity Zinta probably comes to mind—to the exclusion of the crowd of faceless, forgettable film actresses. Because the detail has captured something that cues the *individuality* of the person being described. A creative team is far more likely to create interesting ads if they think they are talking to an interesting person!

(iv) *Profiling the target:* The final watch-out in the area of segmentation and targeting is deciding which elements of the profile of the target person to include in the brief. All too often, the profile in briefs includes too many irrelevant pieces of information about the person. These details are added in order to give a richer picture of the target. But they will achieve this objective only if the details are *relevant to the context of the product and brand.*

Describing Mrs. Kulkarni's household, and how she spends her entire day, and her chores, and all the things she does for the various members of her family may be useful if you are writing a brief for Moov as a backache reliever. But is not of much use if you want the creative team to create an ad for the socks you want her to buy for her kids!

Step 3 then, is to introduce the creative team to the individual with all her quirks and qualities, so that they want to talk to her in an interesting way.

4. CONSUMER UNDERSTANDING

The next step is to think of the reasons that will keep the target you have identified, from buying your brand, and what could motivate them to do so. (Remember that there is very rarely any communication that gets people to actually jump out of their chairs and go rushing off to the store to buy the advertised brand the moment they see the advertising. However, I believe that it must do something, which in the long-term, if not the short-term, builds a positive predisposition to buy your brand. Otherwise the advertising communication has been cheating the advertiser.)

In Chapter 6 we saw six basic barriers, which keep people from buying. To recap these:

o   The target does not feel your offer serves or addresses any of her needs

- ○ She believes she is already getting what she thinks you have to offer, from another product or service
- ○ She does not believe your product or service can deliver what you are promising
- ○ There is some deep-rooted belief or perception which keeps her from accepting what your brand is offering
- ○ There is a poor Performance: Price perception of the offer
- ○ The offer has not generated any buzz

Weigh the evidence carefully and judge which is the critical barrier for your brand. If the basic homework in developing the product has been sound, barrier number 1 should have been taken care of. (Caution: *Should* have been taken care of, does not mean that it *has* been taken care of. It is useful to play the Doubting Thomas and readdress this issue, as a matter of abundant caution if nothing else.)

If the barrier is barrier number 4, chances are that an error has been made in identifying the target segment itself. You may be better off going back, reexamining the information you have, and redefining the segment you wish to address. This is because advertising, or other forms of paid-for communication are not very good at changing basic beliefs and prejudices. These can and may change over time, but usually not fast enough for a brand to benefit.

Here it would be instructive to look at the approaches employed for NECC, during the early 90s, in a campaign with which I was intimately involved. As a cooperative of poultry farmers, the NECC was running a campaign to educate people about the value of consuming eggs. One of the barriers, which restricted egg consumption among a section of the population, was the perception of eggs as a 'non-vegetarian' food item. One of the pieces of communication created was based on the fact that eggs brought to the market from poultry farms are actually *unfertilised* eggs; in that sense they are of animal origin, but one is not consuming 'animal meat' when one eats eggs. In this sense they are comparable to milk, which too is of animal origin. In fact, Mahatma Gandhi had once said that anyone who consumed milk should have no objection to consuming unfertilized eggs. We had created an advertisement, which pointed out this distinction; but people—who held the strong belief that eggs were 'non-vegetarian'—simply did not believe this. It was simply too strong a belief to be swayed by a logical argument.

However, what we discovered was that there *was* a group of people, even among those who held this belief, who—in certain circumstances—would be willing to overcome this belief-barrier to gain the benefits they saw eggs providing. This sub-group comprised pregnant women, or those who were breast-feeding their babies. These women were very conscious that, during this period of their life, they were responsible for meeting the nutritional needs of *two* individuals: themselves and their child! The extra nourishment and nutrition that eggs could add to their diet was thus seen as valuable. During these periods therefore, they were ready to 'put aside' if you will, their belief barrier, and consume eggs.

Figure 10.4: Press advertisement: NECC, for mothers

If there are situations such as this in your product area, you may be able to side-step barrier number 4, by focusing on a context in which the target is willing to override the belief. Yet, by and large, attempting to overcome barrier number 4 is likely to offer a low ROE i.e. Return on Efforts; you are probably better off modifying some other element of the marketing and communication mix so that you can focus on a segment which does not have this barrier to your brand.

Barrier number 3 is one that many marketers believe is the one that needs to be addressed, to create a positive predisposition or preference for a brand. This is what leads to the creation of notions such as 'SGL 4'; this was supposed to be the special ingredient in a shaving cream marketed some years ago, which would give you a smooth shave. The assumption in such cases is that prospects see similarity in the benefits or performance characteristics offered by several brands, and that therefore, the differentiator would be the logic or basis for the performance claims of a particular brand.

An implicit assumption here is also that prospects seek a logical explanation for performance. Recent research studies for FMCG brands however, suggest that as long as basic cues for quality (such as product appearance, packaging, company, etc.) are available, customers take claims as fair statements (with of course the 'natural' discounting of advertising claims that consumers learn to do!), and do not necessarily want details of what 'makes the product tick'. In fact exaggerated attempts to create such magic ingredient or 'reasons why' are likely to reduce, not increase credibility.

So, while there may well be certain situations in which the 'reason why' should be a strong element in your communication, these situations may be relatively few. The real barrier to be tackled in most situations is barrier number 2: the consumer believes she is already getting what she thinks you have to offer, from another product or service.

In all too many situations, the people who are involved with a brand tend to see relatively small differences as significant improvements over other products and brands in the comparison set of the prospect. You may recall the discussion in an earlier chapter about the soft drink concentrate called Trinka—compared to Rasna it was a single liquid concentrate; whereas preparing the Rasna syrup involved a combination of two components—a liquid concentrate and a powder. Consumers, not surprisingly, did not find it a meaningful or significant enough difference to overcome the barrier of 'I already get what you have to offer: convenience and low cost per glass.'

There is evidence that a large proportion of new brands fail, not because customers find the quality unacceptable, or that the product does not perform as expected, but simply because there is nothing different they are seen to offer, due to which *the new brand does not even get tried.*

If you find that your brand is confronting this barrier, it may be necessary to go beyond the left-brain logic of benefits and reasons why and performance differences; to seek differentiation through other routes. We will review previous learnings on these routes shortly.

In the meanwhile, Step 4 in writing the creative brief would be to look at your brand and its competition with ruthless honesty, and identify the barrier it has to overcome. Don't believe that the barrier is a large ditch because you can do the long jump well—the problem may be a hurdle you have to jump over!

5. MOTIVATORS AND DIFFERENTIATORS

The analysis of consumer attitudes, beliefs, opinions, and the potential role of the brand in the prospects' life should have helped you to identify the differentiator and motivator your brand can offer.

5.1: The first thing we need to look at is the level of self-revelation involved in the category or with your brand. Let us go back to the thoughts discussed on this issue in Chapter 7 for a quick recap.

We had seen that there are four levels of personal involvement.

Level 1: 'The Brand does what it is supposed to do.' Very low-level of self-revelation involved. Examples: safety pins, scrubbers, floor cleaners, clothespins, handkerchiefs, socks, kitchen gas lighters.

Level 2: 'The Brand provides personal satisfaction.' Still fairly low level of self-revelation, but choice affects a sense of feeling good. The type of feel-good effect may be:

- *Personal pleasure* as in the choice of biscuit, tea, wafers, etc.
- *Comfort* as in undergarments, shaving razor, etc.
- *Good judgment* as in the selection of health beverage, antiseptic liquid, muscular pain reliever, cough syrup, etc.

Level 3: 'The Brand affects how others see me.' This involves product categories that have a 'badge value'. Categories include watches, clothes, soft drinks, colognes, mobile phones etc. These products are used and in fact on display during their use. The perceptions about the brands in these categories have a bearing on how the user is perceived.

Level 4: 'This is me.' At this level, we are speaking of aspects, which are intensely personal and the brand becomes part of the personal statement and self-identity of the user. These are the brands like Nike, Apple and Ferrari.

5.2: The next thing to consider is the motivator and differentiator the brand can offer and own. Genuinely understanding how the product is used and how it touches the user's life is the key to uncovering the meaningful differentiator. This does not necessarily require large tomes of research; it means being having a real world understanding of the product and brand from the prospects' point of view, without the rose-tinted glasses of the marketing manager's pride in his brand.

6. POSITIONING

Earlier, we discussed that positioning may not be adequate; but do not abandon the effort before you try it. It is possible in many cases that positioning can offer the differentiation for your brand. If your analysis shows that your brand can indeed occupy a unique position, refine this thought further.

Here are examples of some brands, which did manage to find meaningful position-based differentiation in recent times, in spite of a high degree of product parity in their product categories.

Moov: The brand was entering the pain relief market, which had well-entrenched, long-standing brands such as Iodex and Amrutanjan. However, it was able to position itself along the Use-Axis as the *backache reliever,* and could establish itself successfully.

Another brand, which has been successful in recent times, is Ujala. There were several brands in the clothes whitener market, but Ujala, with its memorable *'Char boondon wala'* (Translation: The four-drop one) promise has been able to position itself along the Price-Performance Axis.

7. EMOTIONAL BOND

You must finally consider and, more importantly, choose the basis of the Emotional Bond your brand will go on to establish. We have seen that this can be done using many approaches: from aspects of self-image and identity, values and belief systems, cultural linkages and so on. These are not clearly demarcated optional routes; they are different lenses through which to look at the brand and the prospect so that you can find the basis of a long-term relationship.

Another component of building a relationship with your customer is examining whether your brand can reflect an archetype. Imbuing your brand with the deep, universal qualities embodied in archetypes can build extremely strong relationships with customers.

Remember that the Creative Brief is not a 'Requisition' which the Account Management team or executive issues to the creative team, asking for a supply of the described 'goods'! The brief must be not only a distillate of the analysis you have done, but also distil the judgment of the entire team.

I would urge Account Management teams to develop a 'first cut' of the brief, and use it as the basis for discussion with the creative team. The discussion may well lead to new ways of looking at things, or to the discovery of lacunae in the thinking. Incorporate the output of the discussions into the final cut of the creative brief. The creative brief is not the Ten Commandments—there is nothing wrong with re-writing it! Moreover, by following this process, not only would you have been able to possibly improve the brief, you would also have got the buy-in of the creative team on the approach.

Of course, the *responsibility* for the Creative Brief will always be with the Account Management team. Just as the responsibility for *the final creative output* will be with the creative team.

Chapter 10: Action Point The Creative Brief
Brand: *Product Category:*
1. Directions of market change (Identify the developments in society and the market, which are likely to affect your brand, and whether there are opportunities for your brand to take a leading-edge stance in the market/category. Paint a picture of the emerging reality):
2. Marketing driver and source of business (Identify the factor in your brand mix which has the highest competitive leverage, and the user and usage group which offers the largest potential for your brand.):
3. Segmentation and Targeting (Identify the differentiating characteristics of the *person* you are targeting. Create a picture of the prospect and the aspects of his or her life which the brand will relate to):
4. Key barrier (Identify the key barrier likely to keep prospects from accepting the brand offer):
5. Brand offer or Proposition (Write the statement which reflects the motivator and differentiator, that will overcome the barrier):
6. Positioning intended (This is not mandatory. However, if a positioning opportunity exists, indicate the axis or axes of positioning and where the major competing brands lie on that axis or axes):
7. Emotional Bond & Archetype (Specify the most powerful emotional link you believe the brand can forge with the prospect, and whether the brand can represent an archetype):

CHAPTER 11

Managing a Brand Over Time

Coping with a Dynamic World

Overview

Looking back over the last 30 years, here are some of the changes one might note:

1975: Long hair
2005: Longing for hair

1975: The perfect high
2005: The perfect high yield mutual fund

1975: Rolling Stones
2005: Kidney stones

1975: Being called into the principal's office
2005: Calling the principal's office

1975: Taking acid
2005: Taking antacid

More than ever before, we live in a world in which rapid and unexpected change is the order of the day. These changes in technology, communication media, lifestyles, attitudes, ideas, aspirations and so on result in effects that are not incremental; they mark far more dramatic shifts in the market and social landscape. Obviously these changes impact how people think, what are their priorities, how they form opinions, how they make choices, and thus as consumers—how they spend their time and money.

It is imperative for students and practitioners in the communications profession to study these changes and to understand their implications. In order to manage your brand through these changes it is necessary to look more closely at the particular dimensions of change that impact your brand.

Because creating Power advertising is not a one-time task. It is more in the nature of nurturing a child over a long period, rather than the construction of a wall, which you can more or less forget about, once you have constructed it.

MACRO-DIMENSIONS OF CHANGE

There are several areas of change that are worth noting by everyone who is involved with the managing of brands.

- ○ Perhaps the most obvious one is the sheer explosion in choice. There are dozens of new brands and new variants of older brands in almost any category you look at. Here is a partial list of skin cream and lotion brands and variants launched during 2002.

Afghan Sunscreen
All Fair Natural Freshness
Apsara Blue Shell
Ayur Herbal Winter
Ayur Petroleum Jelly
Ayurvedic Concepts Astringent
Ayurvedic Concepts Fairness Cream
Ayurvedic Concepts Moisturiser
Ayurvedic Concepts Night
Bajaj Boro Herbal
Blue Heaven Face Glow
Bold & Beautiful Fairness Cream
Boro Glow
Borocream
Borodula
Borogreen
Borosoft Special
Borotouch
Cadila Exfoliating Face Wash
Chik Fairee
Chik Tejas
Dr Scholl's
Elovera Spf Sunscreen
Emami Naturally Fair Pearl
Eraser
Eraser Foot Care
Eraser Plus
Everyuth Face Wash
Everyuth Facial Scrub
Fair & Lovely Ayurvedic Cream
Fair & Lovely Body Fairness
Fair & Lovely Dark Circle
Fair & Lovely Freshness Face Wash

Fair & Lovely Reviving
Fairever New Improved
Fairever Silk
Foot Guard Cracked Heel
Gloria Cucumber Gel
Gloria Foam Face Wash
Gloria Mint Gel
Gloria Moisturising Cream
Gloria Under Eye Cream
Himani Gold
Kaveri Fairness Cream
Lakme Balanced Moisturiser
Lakme Fair Perfect
Lakme Golden Glow
Lakme Sunscreen
Lexus Lipguard
Lissome Daily Wear
Lissome Sun Shield
Lotus Aloevera
Lotus Anti Wrinkle
Lotus Cocoa Butter
Lotus Face Wash
Lotus Fairness
Lotus Fruit Pack
Lotus Safe Sun
Lotus Safe Sunscreen
Lotus Sunscreen
Lotus Winter Care
Lux International Skin Cream
Margo Natural
Maybelline Shine Free
No Marks
No Marks Face Pack

Olivea Herbal
Palak Soft & Silky
Pond's All Day Oil-Control
Pond's Daily Face Wash
Pond's Beauty
Pond's Body Lotion
Shade Sunscreen
Spotnil
Synergie Astringent
Synergie Clear Face Wash
Synergie Face Scrub
Synergie Shine Control

Synergie Skin Quenching
Synergie Soothing Eye
Synergie Toner
Synergie Wrinkle Lift
Synergie Wrinkle Lift
Synergie Deep Pore Face Wash
Touch & Glow Gold Moisturiser
Touch & Glow Ivory Moisturiser
Touch & Glow Natural Moisturiser
Touch & Glow Rich Moisturiser
Vaseline Crack Relief
Vicco Turmeric-S

- o Another change that occurred quite rapidly is the change in the perceived value of the 'Imported' label. Not so long ago, people would be thrilled to just receive a couple of cakes of Camay bought for them by a friend returning from a trip abroad. Try keeping a niece happy with that today! Another aspect of the value placed on imported products and brands was reflected in the premium pricing of most imported brands. However, as people have seen foreign brands launched here and actually used them, they have lost this unquestioning sense of awe, and are viewing them as just another set of brands. In fact many international brands have found it necessary to launch low-priced offerings as they learnt that there simply weren't enough takers at the high price points, which they felt were justified by the 'imported' label. Examples of offerings at low or mid-price points by international brands include products from Samsung to LG to Parker to Casio to Nike to McDonalds and more.
- o A third significant change has taken place in attitudes relating to living well. The last generation thought of a house as the culminating achievement of a life well and prudently lived. Today, a 28-year old buys a house with a housing loan. Owners of the Ambassador car used them happily for a decade and more; today a car owner wants to upgrade his car every three years.

Not so long ago, being 'in debt' was anathema. The only situations in which a person would take a loan, was when confronted with issues as important as the education or marriage of a child, or a medical emergency. Today, people in their 20s are quite happy to buy durables, vehicles, and other products on credit or through hire-purchase schemes or to take a personal loan for a holiday abroad.

There are, of course, a host of other changes too, but let us consider in somewhat greater depth, two major societal trends and some specific aspects of change relevant to marketing and communications professionals.

OUR LIVES, ROLES AND RELATIONSHIPS

It is a truism to say that products and brands have to exist in the context of human lives. And among the most basic changes taking place around us, apart from the nuclear family becoming more common, is the change in the roles and relationships among members of families.

First, the urban woman is playing a much more versatile role in the home (apart from the fact that many of her woman friends and relatives are working in part or full-time jobs outside the home). Twenty years ago, her mother would have complained to her husband about the faulty plumbing that needed repair. Today, she calls in the plumber, gets the fault fixed, and chances are that her husband doesn't even ever find out there was a problem.

She is also far more aware of, and involved in the financial decisions of the family. Extensive research by various companies for a host of product categories has shown that there has been a sea change in the life and role of the urban Indian woman in the past few years. As one of these housewives expressed it in a research I was involved with: 'aaj-kal aurat ki duniya badal gayee hai'. (Translation: Nowadays, the world of the woman has changed.) She has emerged from her limited role as the 'housekeeper', to becoming a Home Manager, who not only looks after the family kitchen, she also looks after the children's schoolwork and extra-curricular activities, and manages the home and the household budget.

This change in her role also places her on a more equal footing with her husband; this change in relationship being encouraged by the absence of older *bhabhis* and *devars* (sisters-in-law and brothers-in-law). The equal relationship has had implications for marketers in many categories; in that she is a major influencer of decisions, which were earlier assumed to be taken by the man alone.

We have seen this recognized by makers of consumer durables, where decisions tend to be joint decisions. What about men's garments? We know that the woman plays an important role in the choice of menswear; is there a trick being missed in brands of menswear not targeting the woman?

On the other hand what are the implications of men being more involved in parenting and the upbringing of children?

The establishment of more nuclear families also means that there are more homes with only senior citizens in them. What does this imply for marketers? Is this a segment of consumers who are currently being addressed only by categories such as Medical or other insurance companies and pharmaceutical companies?

THE NEW BALANCE OF POWER

From a marketing and communication perspective, another critical change that has taken place has been the shift in power between buyer and seller, with the buyer firmly in command today. Take a look at some of the areas where the scene has changed forever.

For example, not so long ago, if you wanted a car in a particular colour, you might have had to wait for some time. Today not only are dealers able to offer you the model of your choice off-the-shelf, they are also 'incentivising' you—into buying the vehicle for sure, but also to just take a test-drive. This change in the buyer-seller equation is perhaps most visible in the new retailing formats of supermarkets and departmental stores; from a situation where the customer had a counter between her and the products, she now can touch and feel them and examine them at her pace before making a choice.

A third area of change is the time-shift and space-shift of business. In the earlier system the seller determined the transaction time or hours of business. ('Banking hours 10am to 3pm on Weekdays, and 10am to 1pm on Saturdays'). Today, thanks to ATMs, Phone banking, Internet banking and so on, control of time has passed on to the customer.

An equally significant change has taken place in the notion of the locus of business. There was a time when your office was located at a specified address. Yet, with changes in communication and connectivity, everything is *where you are*; as long as you have your mobile phone, SMS, access to email, voice mail and so on. The implications of this 24X7 connectivity are not all obvious at first glance; and we are yet to see the full impact of this change.

For instance: what does it mean for a provider of pest-control services, if the service personnel can no longer say, 'Sir you were not at home when we called to confirm the appointment'—because you would say, 'So why didn't you just call me on my mobile phone?'

Think how it would affect an express delivery service, if you could leave instructions with them saying, 'Just call me tomorrow when a package I am expecting from London arrives—and I shall tell you where I shall be, and where I would like you to deliver it'.

There are several other examples of the shift in the balance of power from the seller to the buyer.

'No questions asked' return policies offered by retailers.

Auctioning of airline tickets on the Internet.

Figure 11.1: Press advertisement: BNP Paribas, off-branch banking services

'Order over the phone' and 'Home delivery' service provided by your local grocery store, florist and even your vegetable seller!

MICRO-DIMENSIONS OF CHANGE

Apart from these areas of change that have altered the marketing landscape, there are going to be a number of changes that will take place more and more frequently, at a micro level; and these will affect specific brands even more dramatically. Let us look at some of these aspects of change.

1. CHANGING COMPETITIVE REFERENCE POINTS

With increasing numbers of brands in almost every product category, this is bound to be the arena of greatest change. This requires that brands must have both a long-term vision of what the core of the brand is and what it stands for; but equally must be agile enough to deal with specific developments in the short-term.

The soap wars

In the 1970s Surf represented the best a washing product could get. It represented high quality, was priced higher than other washing products and had almost no 'direct' competition (although there were other brands of blue detergent available, such as Swastik, Point, Sway and so on). In the 1980s a landmark event, one that everyone in marketing and advertising is aware of, took place in the area of washing products: Nirma was launched—at about one-third the price of Surf.

At one level, this was not even 'competition' when viewed through the window of competition being defined as approximately similarly priced products. However, it revolutionised the business, and created a market that was several hundred thousand tonnes in size. It also led to a practice, where some housewives washed their regular, ordinary clothes in Nirma and their more expensive, delicate clothes in Surf. So much so that Surf found itself forced into responding to Nirma. The most well-known form of this response was the series of Lalitaji TV commercials in which the lady compared the two (without mentioning Nirma), and pointed out that: '*Sasti cheez aur achhi cheez mein fark hota hai*' (Translation: There is a difference between a cheap thing and a good thing).

The effort did not stop the growth of Nirma, and it was not until Wheel was launched that the makers of Surf had an effective challenger to Nirma. But something else had happened in the meanwhile: when you compare two things, *people will assume that they are in fact comparable.*

In some ways Surf had allowed itself to be drawn into Nirma's arena. So when Ariel was introduced, it was the first compact detergent, and represented the new generation of washing product. In some ways the battle with Nirma in which Surf was engaged, left an empty place at the top of the washing product totem pole, which Ariel could occupy.

Surf had been caught in the shift of competing reference points.

You can *beat a Bajaj*

A somewhat similar change in the competitive reference points affected Bajaj Auto, the undisputed leader in two-wheelers for years. In fact the dominance of the Bajaj brand in two-wheelers was so complete, that there was more than a grain of truth in the tag-line that Bajaj used to use in its advertising: You just can't beat a Bajaj.

However, as things turned out, someone could.

Until the early eighties, scooters and motorcycles were seen as significantly different products. The former were better than motorcycles in fuel economy, with a lower initial investment, easier to ride by women. The latter were seen as 'manly' vehicles, not suitable for women, less fuel-efficient than scooters, more expensive in terms of initial cost, and not very safe.

Bajaj scooters (they did not make motorcycles in any significant numbers at that time) competed with other scooters: made by LML, Kinetic Honda, and so on. And beat them hands down.

With the launch of the 4-stroke Hero Honda 100cc motorbike however, things suddenly changed. With a fuel economy of 80 km to the litre, it promised that you could just 'Fill it. Shut it. Forget it.'

With that one promise, the two-wheeler business changed completely. Motorcycles became far more widely accepted; and Hero Honda eventually toppled Bajaj from the top spot in two-wheelers.

That was yet another case of the change in competitive reference point, changing things radically for a brand.

2. CHANGES IN CONSUMER PREFERENCES

Changing tastes and preferences is another phenomenon that can radically affect brands.

One of the major changes in the last decade and a half has been a change in preference from 'strong' or 'heavy' to 'light'. This is a consequence of the concern for health, although of course this is more evident in some categories than others. One of the categories where this has been seen quite strongly is that of edible oil. There has been a definite shift in consumer preference from heavier oils such as mustard and groundnut oil, to lighter oils such as sunflower and soya. In fact now, sunflower makes up about half the total packaged edible volume sold in India.

One brand which was launched on the platform of being anti-cholesterol, 'good for your heart' was Saffola, a safflower oil. For many years, it was promoted for heart patients and almost like a medical product. With the change in preferences and more widespread concerns about heart and stress related problems, the brand was able to move to preventive usage, and then through the introduction of blends, into the area of general health.

A similar preference shift from strong to light led to smokers moving away from the raw, strong taste of unfiltered brands of cigarettes such as Panama and Charminar (once the largest selling brand of cigarettes in India.) This trend has been noted across the world, and many cigarette brands introduced low-tar or mild variants, which have become larger sellers than the earlier 'regular' variants. However, the brand Charminar was perhaps too strongly associated with its strong taste and even though variants of the brand were introduced, they were unable to help the brand make the transition and gain acceptance in the context of changed consumer preferences.

3. ASPIRATIONS AND REFERENCE GROUPS

The portrayal of certain types of personalities and the use of certain endorsers are common means of creating aspiration imagery for brands. Yet, these types, too, are not eternal. They too are subject to change.

Until the early 1980s, the image of the perfect male, most commonly visible in textile advertising reflected the classical definition of manhood: the men were all, tall, dark, handsome, very masculine, strong of jaw, aloof, imperious. Of course they were all successful. The beautiful woman by his side was a trophy, no less than his expensive car or his fancy house or prize-winning thoroughbred horse.

But there was a wind of change blowing slowly, and the first brand to reflect the change was perhaps Raymond. It introduced us to 'The Complete Man'—sensitive, understanding, not unwilling to show emotion, attractive but not offensively handsome. And he was a friend to the woman in his life.

The complete man was the next male stereotype in advertising in India for many years, until the 'knowledge economy' became a reality. Now, not only is the man sensitive and caring, he also wears spectacles as befits his intelligence; and his props are more likely to be a briefcase, a laptop computer or a PDA, than a riding crop or a rifle!

And with the dressing down ushered in by the internet era, there was a change which was celebrated by Allen Solly as it introduced the notion of 'Friday Dressing'. Allowing men to wear maroon and yellow and other brightly coloured shirts instead of the boring old pastel shades to work.

If there have been changes in the male myth, the changes have been no less dramatic in the female of the species.

Femina has long been the standard-bearer for the woman who sought independence and wanted to establish her own identity. In the early 1980s she ventured away from the familiar comfort of her home, learned to live alone, to cope with life and career challenges, and emerged as a woman of substance.

Over time, more and more urban women (especially in the metro cities and in mini-metros) began to take these ideas of independence and self-confidence for granted. These were no longer images of aspiration; they were merely reflections of their day-to-day lives.

Figure 11.2: Press advertisement: *Femina,* **'Woman of Substance'**

Femina too changed, in response to these changes as the aspirational woman moved further away from the traditional mould (the changes in *Femina* were aided and abetted by the arrival of magazines such as *Cosmopolitan* and *Elle*, and TV shows such as *Saans*). She was now ready to accept her sexuality, did not feel compelled to stay on in a failed marriage, discovered single-parenthood and did not always need a man to escort her to a party.

The new *Femina* (Figure 11.3) has moved from supporting the woman of substance to reflecting Generation *W*.

TOMORROW'S PEOPLE

In a somewhat related area, there has been a huge change in what interests girls as they are growing up. Among the interests, perhaps even expectations, of a girl some years ago, were knitting, stitching and sewing. This, of course, meant that many of them wanted a sewing machine at home. With the changes in aspirations, far fewer girls are interested in knitting, sewing, and so on. The effect of this change in interests is noticeable: do you recall the last time you saw an ad for sewing machines on TV?

These and several other changes are compelling a host of Indian companies to confront changes in tastes, in lifestyles, and aspirations; changes in

Figure 11.3: Press advertisement: *Femina,* 'Generation *W*'

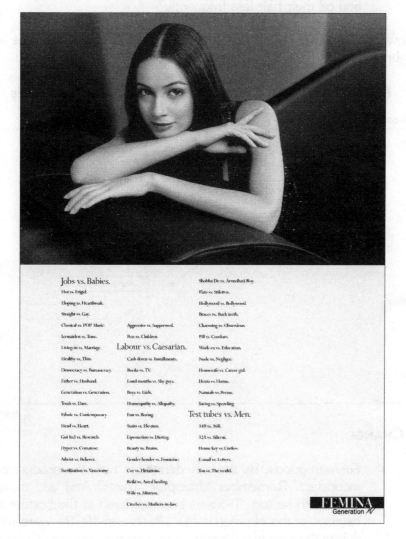

competitive reference frames and changes in technology in their categories. Here are some of them. Put yourself in the shoes of the managers of these brands: how would you deal with the challenges they face?

- What should a manufacturer of dress materials like Garden do, as more and more girls prefer to buy readymade clothes?
- How does a maker of soft drink concentrate deal with an increasing preference, even among young kids, for bottled beverages?

○ What does a brand of hair oil do as women turn to shorter hair and oil their hair less frequently?

However there will clearly be a difference in the *rate of change* across categories.

Figure 11.4: Time and change in different product categories

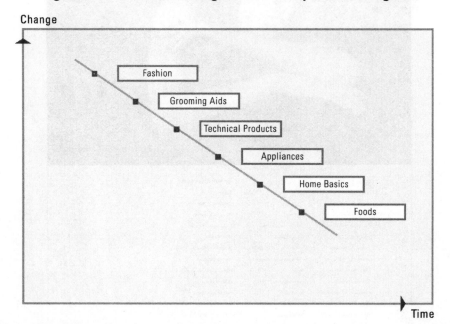

RATE OF CHANGE

○ *Fashion goods:* By the very definition, here the product itself is inconstant! Remember 'drainpipe' pants? And yet, there is a cycle to these too. Trousers became flared at the bottom in the heydays of the Hippies in the 1960s and 1970s, were rejected during the next two decades, and have now become flared at the bottom again.

And of course, designers consciously make the previous versions of the 'product' obsolete by introducing seasonal collections with much fanfare.

○ *Grooming aids:* This area too tends to be strongly culture-based, and changes with the changes in lifestyles and taste preferences. Hair colour, hair gel, make-up—all of these are handmaidens to fashion and are also subject to short life cycles. For example, consider how with the changes in the associations evoked by denim, a brand of men's toiletries like 'Denim' seems to be outdated today.

- o *Technology products:* In technology categories, change is often discontinuous, which can change the market itself. Think of the shifts from audio cassettes to CDs to now MP3 players in music.

  Or the changes from video cassettes to VCDs to DVDs.

- o *Appliances:* Changes in this area are more incremental. How much has the simple household iron changed in the last 20 years? How different can a toaster get? The significant changes that take place in this category are likely to be on account of discontinuous technologies. Take, for example, CFC-free refrigerants; or flat screen TVs, or, now, plasma TV. Or, for that matter, the introduction of microwave ovens.

- o *Home basics:* This covers categories such as floor cleaners, bathroom cleaners, polish. In these cases, the peripherals (e.g. delivery system of a simple bottle changing to a spray pump) probably change more than the basic product

- o *Foods:* Changes in preferences and the acceptance of new products in foods is far slower than in most other categories. While several new categories of packaged food have been launched in the last few years, very few have gained widespread acceptance. The ones that have been accepted are mainly packaged forms of common foods such as pickles and cooking *masalas*. It is well known that Kelloggs has waited for many years for food habits to change in some markets, so the resistance to change in food habits is not unique to India.

MANAGING CHANGE

Femina managed to deal with change and has remained relevant. Charminar failed to manage change and is fading away. Here are some examples of other brands coping with change. Think about whether there are parallels with your brand. And whether there are lessons to be drawn from what these brands did, which could benefit your brand.

Eat healthy. Think better.

Britannia is a house brand with a host of product brands. Britannia Marie, Thin Arrowroot, Milk Bikis were just some of the product brands the company had until the early 1990s. Britannia not only had a range of biscuits in the market, its product range also included rolls, cakes and bread.

Some of these offered the pleasure of indulgence; others were tasty snacks, yet others offered nutrition and health. Many of these sub-brands were supported independently, and there was little or no synergy across the range. It was also becoming inefficient and infeasible to support all the products in the range.

A wide-ranging review of the range, and extensive research was carried out to find a strong unifying thread across the full range. This search for a unifying thread led the company to the 'Eat healthy, Think better' concept (actually the concept is probably expressed better in Hindi, with the line '*Swasth khao, Tan-man jagao*'), with a new logo for Britannia, and the new line 'Eat healthy, Think better' which was carried on to the packaging for all products.

Figure 11.5: Logo: Britannia, the new logo

Yet, it must be noted that this was not merely a case of adopting a new logo and line—that would have been a cosmetic change without any substantiation. A change of logo and line, which expresses a new thought to consumers must be accompanied by action which prove the brand's commitment to the new thought. Britannia went beyond the logo change, and actually changed the product range. Some products such as the jelly-filled rolls, which offered no nutritional value, were dropped from the range. Others, which did not have strong health benefits, were fortified with nutritional ingredients—such as the reformulated Marie Gold. Yet others were reformulated and re-named, such as Thin Arrowroot becoming Nutri Choice; and, finally, new brands such as Tiger, firmly built on a nutrition-giving formulation were launched.

Figure 11.6: Packaging: Britannia, change in product and packaging

Moreover, the brand's commitment to the new platform was communicated through a campaign, which celebrated the new concept. Everything the brand did conveyed the seriousness of the brand in effecting a change; it was not just a question of releasing a new campaign.

Lifebuoy hai jahan...(where there's Lifebuoy...)

For over a century, Lifebuoy—the world's largest selling soap, has meant a familiar brick-red soap with a distinctive carbolic smell, and the promise of germ-free health. The *'Tandurusti ki raksha karta hai Lifebuoy...'* (Translation: Lifebuoy protects your health...) jingle is familiar to generations of Indians. And yet, the giant was tiring as the new millennium began.

In 2002 Lifebuoy was re-launched. Lifebuoy was no longer the carbolic soap; it turned into regular (milled) toilet soap, with a new health fragrance. It had a new formulation. And it targeted the housewife seeking health protection for her family, a significant move away from the sporty, active, male world of health to a softer, warmer, world of health for the entire family.

Not only has the basic toilet soap undergone a huge change, the brand has been extended to other variants and products, which have extended the germ-fighting associations of the brand to a variety of situations and applications. Lifebuoy International Plus fights germs, which cause body odour. Lifebuoy International Gold helps protect against germs, which cause skin blemishes.

Through a re-interpretation of 'health' expressed again, as in the case of Britannia, through changes in the product, backed by communication efforts, the brand has reinvented itself and is one of Hindustan Lever's major success stories in the past few years. A brand, which is over 100 years old, has been rejuvenated to become a brand that is sprightly and youthful. While staying true to the core of what the brand stands for: daily health through protection against germs.

Figure 11.7: Press advertisement: Lifebuoy, protection against germs

Saffola. The heart of a healthy brand

Saffola was the first cooking oil to focus sharply on a health benefit; it addressed people who were suffering from heart-related problems. Launched over 35 years ago, the brand is widely recognized by consumers to be 'Good for the Heart'. Initially, the sharp focused approach of the brand helped it to establish a clearly differentiated, meaningful position for itself. However, over time, this specialization itself became a limitation, as people who did not see themselves as 'having a heart problem' saw no reason to use it.

Saffola undertook a major re-positioning exercise in 1993. The repositioning was based on a significant change that was taking place in urban India: the fact that urban males under the age of 40 was the fastest growing segment of Indian heart patients. And that even people who did not 'have heart problems', were at risk due to stress, smoking and so on.

Saffola moved from being the brand you use when you have a heart problem, to the one you use to prevent it. The repositioning (Figure 11.8) gave the brand a tremendous new momentum as it brought in a whole set of new users, conscious of the risks of the high-stress, high-flying life they were leading.

Figure 11.8: Press advertisement: Saffola, aimed at people who run the risk of heart problems

The brand undertook yet another step in managing change in 1998, with the adoption of 'Heart of a Healthy Family' as its tag line, and a new heart-shaped jar (Figure 11.9).

In the third move, in 2002, a variant based on a blend of safflower oil with rice bran oil Saffola Nutri Blend, was introduced as the brand continued its efforts to expand the consumer base of Saffola. The variant offered good health for the entire family, as increasing health consciousness among young urban families created an opportunity for a healthier cooking medium at a reasonable cost.

There was of course the question of whether the brand was now moving too far away from its core. From 'heart care for those who have heart problems' to 'care for the heart for those at risk of heart problems' might be an extension of the franchise that is valid. Yet, the line between *extending the core strength of a brand to grow the franchise* and *spreading it too thin* is a fine one that brand custodians must watch carefully. Can the brand retain its core—and more importantly, its uniqueness, as it moves to general family health? Or will it now start becoming close to Sundrop the sunflower oil, which also states that it is 'The healthy oil for healthy people'?

The managers of the brand answered the questions posed above in 2004, with a return to the core of the brand's equity (Figure 11.10).

Figure 11.9: TV commercial: Saffola, 'family health'

...Sona nahin, khona nahin. Sehat se jeena hai. A girl is seen exercising in her home.

A little girl giggles uncontrollably on being tickled by her dad. FVO: *Dhoka nahin, badla nahin...*

The shot of a man out for a brisk jog. FVO states in the background, *Rukna nahin, thakna nahin...*

Cut to a woman, practising yoga. The FVO continues: *Bandhna nahin, baandhna nahin, Shikaayat nahin...*

A young mother proudly holds her toddler. FVO: *Koi compromise nahin. Aansoon nahin, andhera nahin.*

As the family settles down for a barbecue luncheon, the MVO adds, *Saffola swasth parivaar ke dil ki dhadkan.*

...*Sehat se jeena hai.* The shot of a healthy old couple smiling into the camera. *Dar nahin, deewar nahin...*

Cut to family out on a picnic. The kids scamper around and enjoy themselves. Jingle: *Mujhe rehna hai swasth.*

Figure 11.10: TV commercial: Saffola (2004), return to the 'heart' of its equity

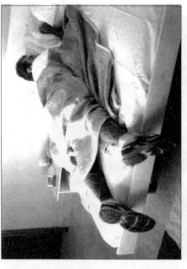

She finds that he has gone back to lie down on the bed after putting on his shoes

New day…their little son is riding the exercycle which is meant for the husband, while the latter is relaxing. Jingle: "From tomorrow…"

Wife peeps into room to see if her husband is ready to go for his jog

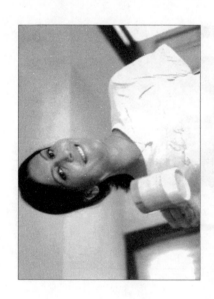

Yet she smiles, thinking he will start jogging from the next day onwards

Yet another day, and she espies the husband tucking into street food....

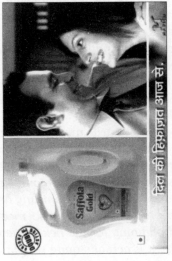

दिल की हिफ़ाज़त आज से.

They look happy and healthy. VO: Care for the heart. Starting today.

Wife gets upset and worried about him ignoring his health....

She then realizes she *has* to do something...and buys Saffola. VO: He always talks about doing something *tomorrow*...You can do something from today.

Summing Up

In a world and marketplace where change is the only constant, managing a brand through changing times will be the greatest challenge for brand custodians.

The drivers of change will come from many sources: the media, peer influences and opinion leaders, technology. And they shape our desires, attitudes, role models, aspirations, concerns and lifestyles. They affect culture, peer norms, taboos.

To manage change, we must change from being reactive, from projecting the past into the future. Instead, we must look ahead, discern the emerging shape of things to come and own the shape of the trend. This means you must lead the change, not merely follow or reflect it.

And, sometimes, it will mean you—yourself—making your product obsolete before someone else does. The best examples of this are visible in the new generations of chips that Intel introduces to replace their own earlier designs; it is visible in the new versions of operating systems that Microsoft and Apple introduce; it is visible in the newer models of mobile phones that Nokia, Samsung and others introduce.

At a more practical level, it also means involving leading edge groups in market research, and planning for the next generation of customers.

In principle, it is actually quite simple. Strategically, all that we must manage are:

- *The target*
- *The offer*
- *The expression of that offer*

So that the brand and the unique, emotionally compelling set of associations evoked by the name remain meaningful even as the ebb and flow of time takes place.

It is really quite simple, isn't it?

Simple; but not easy.

Therein lies the challenge. And the reward of planning for Power Advertising.

MUST-READ BOOKS ON ADVERTISING

Ten books that contain exceptional left-brain *and* right-brain logic about brands and advertising:

Managing Brand Equity
by David A. Aaker

Building Strong Brands
by David A. Aaker

Ogilvy on Advertising
by David Ogilvy

Strategic Brand Management
by Jean-Noel Kapferer

Positioning: The Battle for Your Mind
by Al Ries, Jack Trout

And Now a Few Words From Me: Advertising's Leading Critic Lays Down the Law, Once and For All
by Bob Garfield

Inventing Desire: Inside Chiat/Day : The Hottest Shop, the Coolest Players, the Big Business of Advertising
by Karen Stabiner

The Hero and the Outlaw: Building Extraordinary Brands Through the Power of Archetypes
by Margaret Mark, Carol S. Pearson

A New Brand World: Eight Principles for Achieving Brand Leadership in the 21st Century
by Scott Bedbury, Stephen Fenichell

Truth, Lies and Advertising: The Art of Account Planning
by Jon Steel

Index